Crossing the Bridge

Crossing the Bridge

A practitioner's learning journey into systems thinking and Creating the Conditions for Change

Pauline Roberts

Edited by: Louise Bond

Crossing the Bridge

A practitioner's learning journey into systems thinking and Creating the Conditions for Change

Pauline Roberts

Edited by: Louise Bond

Dedication

For my sisters, Sue and Janet.

You may not be able to read this book,
but I know you are with me every step of the way.

Table of Contents

Table of Figures

Acknowledgements

When I first set out on my journey to apply systems thinking in my work situations, many around me did not know where I was going with it or what I would do with it. Indeed, neither did I. They tirelessly walked alongside me anyway. Some of them have been with me for years, giving me guidance and encouragement in just the right amount, at the right time.

It is difficult to individually thank everyone who has played a part in my journey. The kindness directed towards me from the sidelines has, at times, been overwhelming. The friends who never gave up on me, the neighbour who encouraged me, the work colleague who championed me, the student who gave me a high five after a lecture, the other students who let me be a part of their life for a while, the manager who wholeheartedly believed in me, the family member who probably still doesn't understand me, the person in the pub, the stranger in a coffee shop, the woman I met on the tube, with whom I talked for only 10 minutes and yet we bonded closely over shared ideas and values. All have inspired me in one way or another. If you are reading this and we have met and you have encouraged me in some way, you are on this list.

I thank you all for your dedication and commitment to supporting me and for your wisdom and inspiration. Without it, I never would have made it to this point.

Love and best wishes,

Pauline

Introduction

A note from the author

Have you ever felt like you are drowning in the overwhelming complexity that surrounds you in your work situations? Complexity that makes you feel like you have a bridge to cross but the wooden slats of the footway are old and rotten and some are no longer attached to the rest of the construction? There is no other way around, you have to cross the bridge. The bridge with frayed rope handrails, which have seen better days, and you are not even sure if they are securely attached to the riverbank on the other side. The bridge that sways mercilessly every time you move your weight forward. It has a menacingly gushing river below it, waiting to welcome you into its perilous white-water turmoil. I have felt like this several times throughout my career. It happens every time I start a new job, take on a new, large project and whenever I am faced with what seems like unfathomable complexity. It can be anxiety-inducing, to say the least.

I felt like this when I entered the world of National Health Service (NHS) commissioning. It was unchartered territory for me, and my task was to navigate the fast-paced and challenging area of urgent care. I had never commissioned before and I was not even sure what urgent care meant when I started the job. The organisation I worked for was grappling with winter pressures, high demand for hospital beds and debilitating delays in hospital discharge. I knew there was a challenge ahead. I felt the same way when I stepped into systems thinking consultancy for the first time. Again, it was unchartered territory with new and unique challenges I had never faced before.

On both occasions, despite the odds stacked against me, I decided that backwards was not a feasible direction, so across the bridge I had to go. It was on the bridge that I faced my greatest work fears. What if I wasn't sure where to start? Would I give bad advice? How would I move things forwards? How would I convince people that my ideas were appropriate? Did I even have the legitimacy to make a change?

It was on the bridge that I learnt and iteratively developed my systems practice. I became a systems thinking practitioner by being brave enough to step onto the treacherous rotten wooden slats. By allowing myself to feel vulnerable and exposed and yet still trying out the approaches, methods, models and ideas. By forcing myself to take deeply considered risks and by allowing myself to frequently fail. There were many times that my foot went straight through the rotting wood and I had to grasp the rope handrails and cling on for dear life. There were times when I slipped and fell face down, seeing the rapid white water below zooming towards me, only to regain my composure and save myself from a fatal mistake at the last minute. I continued to navigate the perils of the bridge with determination to get to the other side.

Every time I cross the bridge I develop and refine my systems practice. It is on the bridge where I learn my craft. It is where I experiment. It is where I learn how to teach the theory to others. It is an iterative and challenging journey. Each time, the experience remains the same – precarious, shaky and fear-inducing. I have come to realise that this is not a bad thing. It is just a thing. It is a way of learning. I slip, I fall, my foot goes down a hole, and I get rope burns on my palms. Then, I find my footing, navigate the complexity, slat by rotting slat, and eventually step off the other side of the bridge onto a velvet-like carpet of calming grass.

It is on the bridge where the systems thinking practitioner in me is created. It is on the bridge where I fail, succeed, learn, fail, and succeed again. It is the learning from my story of crossing the bridge that I would like to share with you. I hope that if you too are crossing the systems practice bridge, this book reassures you about your journey. I hope that if you have never crossed the systems practice bridge before, you might be tempted to take your first tentative steps.

I believe that every systems thinking practitioner's learning journey as they cross the bridge is valid and important, no matter their experiences. I believe it is this narrative of our own experiences, captured in our own words, that is often lost, never having been recorded. In sharing my journey of crossing the bridge, I extend my hand and invite you onto the bridge. One day, I hope you too, share your learning journey with the rest of us.

The systems thinking kaleidoscope

A word for those who are not too familiar with systems thinking. I describe it as a way of thinking about situations using the concept of a system. It is a way of exposing things that help us learn about the situation so that we can identify how to make improvements or changes. Systems, in my perspective, are learning devices. Applying systems thinking is about learning.

When people talk about systems, you tend to hear words like constructs, interdependencies, interconnectivity, perspectives or complexity. The ideas can sound technical and off-putting. But think of it like putting a different lens up to your eyes. It involves learning how to understand situations more deeply and in different ways. You also learn about yourself and your impact on and in those situations at the same time.

Engaging with systems thinking is like putting your eye up to a child's kaleidoscope. At first, you only see a jumbled mess of brightly coloured pieces of plastic lurking in the distance. But then, with a little shake or a twist, an awe-inspiring, vibrant pattern emerges, large as life, as if by astonishing magic.

As the pattern emerges, I get a profound sense of the challenges as giant brick walls and the opportunities as transparent flowing rivers, trickling over smooth patterned stones. I see how flexible people and their organisations or community groups are now and how adaptable they might need to be in the future to enable something different to happen.

As a systems thinking practitioner, I do not just look at things in a situation, but at the interactions between things and what happens because of the interactions. Rather than analysing parts of a situation separately, I focus on synthesising my understanding of what is happening. I explore what obstructs, disrupts, delays, diverts, supports and encourages people's efforts to make improvements.

I explore purposes and identity, interconnections and interdependencies. I focus on perceptions, projections, framing and biases, behaviours, assumptions and communication. I look at interactions, influences and relationships. I probe boundaries and explore how people collaborate and reciprocate.

Systems thinking helps me understand why decisions that made sense at one point in time may no longer be appropriate and why we might need to do something different now. I explore at both a macro and micro level to gain an understanding of the wider context in which the situation is embedded, constantly zooming out and in, out and in.

In short, the systems thinking I embody in my systems practice is a way of looking at and engaging with complex situations. It is a way that has the potential to open me and others up to new possibilities that we might never have previously contemplated.

It is important to say at this point, that everyone's systems practice is different. You could have ten practitioners in a room, and they might each have a different perception of systems thinking and how they engage with it. What I talk about in this book is how I perceive systems thinking and how I embody my own systems practice. It is my learning journey as I iteratively cross the bridge to develop my craft.

Who should read this book?

This book should appeal to you if you are a fellow systems thinking practitioner and are interested in another practitioner's journey. You may be an aspiring practitioner and want to hear more about what it is like to step fully into the arena. Perhaps you are a student of systems thinking and want to hear more about the reality of putting systems thinking into practice. Maybe you are trying out systems thinking approaches for the first time and need some reassurance about your journey. Or you may be an interested party, dipping into something because it sounds interesting. This book is for everyone, in equal measure.

This book is not heavily technical or academic. It is the story of a learning journey and is designed for people who want to engage with the discipline on the ground themselves or hear about what that is like.

My style of systems practice has been well received by people working in public services, charitable organisations and those working on place-based systems change in equal measure.

If you are aspiring to 'create the conditions for change' in your work situations, you will find practical guidance to help you on your way.

How to use this book

This book is written in four distinct parts. The first part is about the formative years of my systems practice. It is written in the style of a memoir of my experiences.

The second part is about my ever-evolving approach to creating the conditions for change. It is based on my personal learning from putting Stafford Beer's Viable System Model (VSM) and other systems thinking approaches into practice. It is focused on leadership and systems leadership and is particularly useful in public services and place-based systems change. It has a focus on bringing humanity back into situations and harnessing the gifts and wisdom of all of those involved.

Part three is about the practitioner's journey. It is here that I consider common themes that I, and other practitioners, go through on our learning journeys. I do not cover everything that happens to us along the way but there are some patterns I hear about repeatedly. They are usually the things that newer practitioners think only happen to them because they are just learning. I wish someone had told me when I started out that they are normal, common and likely to be with you for the duration of your journey.

The final part of this book is where I contemplate the way forward for my systems practice. Where now? And why?

It is easy to dip into and out of each of these parts in isolation. Of course, if you want to gain the full picture of where my ideas came from, reading from cover to cover would give a broader picture. Reading the parts in isolation will still make for interesting reading, depending upon your area of interest – the formative years of my systems practice, the approach I currently use, common themes of a practitioner's journey and contemplating a way forward for the future.

Part 1: The foundations of my systems practice

Pauline Roberts

Chapter 1: An emerging craft

It is the middle of lockdown during the first wave of Covid-19 in the UK, 2020. I am at my home computer running a series of workshops with a group of people working on systems change. We are playing around with systems thinking tools and techniques, talking about living systems, power, labels and imposter syndrome. We are experimenting with storytelling and prototyping. It had been a full and invigorating programme running over six months. I feel overwhelmed and momentarily amazed. I feel radiantly warm inside, relaxed, and secretly hopeful. The most recent part of my perpetually undulating system practice journey had been emotional. I never imagined I would engage with groups of people in different online meeting rooms, and we would do such powerful work together.

In this phase of my journey, I supported several projects focused on systems change. I worked with groups immersed in place-based systems change in different geographical areas, charitable organisations working together to make a change, groups from primary care in the UK National Health Service (NHS) looking for a different way forward, and groups of established business consultants seeking to enhance their capabilities to support others. They were all different from one another and yet similar, at the same time.

The people were authentic and grounded. In our sessions, they worked from the heart with passion and humility. In each case, we came together as a group who had never met before. We left as a group who experienced vulnerability, trepidation, fondness and an appreciation for each other and our interconnected situations. We formed honest and deep reciprocal relationships which brought a comforting sense of humanity into the online spaces we occupied together.

The people I met at this stage of my journey were positive and passionate about creating change. They openly shared their real-world experiences. I heard gritty, heart-wrenching stories about the challenges of everyday life. We were online because of the Covid-19 lockdowns and the necessity to work in different ways.

A human touch, online

Working online with people was a revelation. I found it liberating not to have to travel for two to four hours to do my work. I was in the comfort of my own home, and I felt extremely relaxed. From the body language in the groups, others felt comfortable and relaxed too. Cats were welcome, dogs were welcome, and, indeed encouraged. If people's children made an appearance, that was fine too. People could be in their living rooms, their kitchens, and sometimes their bedrooms. As long as they were comfortable, it was all fine with me. I liked it. I liked seeing people in their real surroundings, not hiding behind their chain mail work camouflage, with their true selves hidden behind the obscuring armour.

In the sessions, we grappled with Zoom fatigue and online platform anxiety. We dealt with having to look at our own faces on camera. We were relaxed about internet drop-outs, and we fumbled around with the complex world of online interactive whiteboards and tools. We were learning a way forward together, bonding through our vulnerabilities. It made our sessions feel authentic, rather than a staged attempt at perfection. It was an unexpected positive, deepening our relationships. Most of all, engaging with such a wide variety of groups opened up a world of honest and satisfying connections. I saw a painless blending of learning, work, and home life in a beautiful symbiotic relationship that was accepted by all. I welcomed every element of it and so did most of the people in the groups, with arms and hearts wide open, with acceptance and mutual consideration for each other's situations.

What was it that enabled these wholesome connections? One thing that levelled the playing field was that on screen, up came our name. It was not a work title, but a name. Our name. No cliques were standing in corners of rooms. No conversations with one or two individuals, excluding others. There were no huddles by the toilets, leaving people out.

You may think these are the things that are missing when we have online interactions, and these informal face-to-face encounters and chats are vital. That might be the case sometimes, but it is not always the case. Online, extroverts have fewer opportunities to dominate. Introverts have the chance to contribute. Those in higher hierarchical positions may be in their kitchens or living rooms, bringing a human element to their presence, tumbling them from their pedestal.

In my opinion, the world of online interaction brought lots of warmth that was often missing in work meeting rooms or face-to-face workshop scenarios. It removed the labels we are often saddled with, and we came to the party as people. Just people. The people I met brought their vulnerable selves, their confident selves, their unsure selves, their worried selves, their exhausted selves, their excited selves, their authentic selves. They brought their version of reality and coupled it with a desire to share. We shared and laughed and at times, we cried. We laughed some more, cried some more and kept learning our way forward together. The constraining, formal suits of power that people might have worn in the workplace dissolved as we tapped into our inner selves and shed the camouflaged skins in which we usually hid every day. We were creating the conditions that allowed us to explore together, learn together and consider how we might make change together.

If you are familiar with my work, you may have heard me claim that people who do not identify as systems thinkers or even know what system thinking is, often happen to be some of the strongest and most insightful systems thinkers I know. Those people certainly came out to play in these online sessions. I came across people with an inner, determined, and yet virtually unconscious perseverance in the face of adversity that enabled them to observe the world differently and think differently. It enabled them to engage with situations from a multitude of perspectives. Their natural skills repeatedly impressed me.

The key attributes of the insightful, thoughtful people in the groups were that they demonstrated humility and a sense of inner confidence and strength. This was not the first time I had experienced this. It was a recurring theme throughout my work, and here it was again, large as life. Many had the humility to self-reflect and not to jump to making judgements about others. They could connect and form relationships. They were willing to embrace not knowing and were eager to explore. They were empathetic. The majority of the sessions oozed with empathy. So much so that it was difficult for me to deal with personally, sometimes. I tend to readily absorb the energy around me so had to protect myself from becoming overwhelmed.

I heard touching stories of blockages and barriers to social support that are built into the fabric of our society. Blockages and barriers that take away people's dignity and mercilessly throw them to the ground. I heard stories of passionate workers who refused to give in and determinedly navigated an unimaginably complex web of crippling bureaucracy to support others. I heard stories of people who realised that they were indeed leaders, even though they were not at the top of the hierarchy in their organisation. I heard stories of Aha! moments, of finding different ways of having conversations, and of self-belief, particularly when people realised their frustrations were legitimate.

It was overwhelming stuff, and the people I engaged with articulated it and considered how they might work positively with it. Humility, humanity, embracing vulnerability, forming constructive relationships, supporting others, taking selfless actions, engaging positively and truly caring, were at the forefront.

It can be challenging to engage in this way in a world that appears to encourage division, unfairness, discrimination, and at times, hatred. I will often remind people not to underestimate how difficult it can be to embrace their vulnerability, to have self-belief, to nurture relationships with others and indeed, with themselves. It can take courage to be authentic and explore our identity and purposes. Real courage does not always come easily.

But why were these human elements so prominent in the work? Why were we not just focusing on a series of steps to make a change? When exploring a situation with a systems thinking lens, unfolding and embracing what it means to be human is key for me. I never forget that it is people we are engaging with. People come to these situations with all of the doubts and desires, fears and hopes, loves and hates, setbacks and ambitions that we all experience. Is it any surprise that these things have become central to my systems practice?

Actually, yes. It was a surprise for me. I did not go easily into this arena, which I originally perceived as a dense and seemingly impenetrable forest. I stood at the periphery for a long time, peering into deep darkness, frightened to venture into the closely interwoven matrix. I saw pitch-black shadows and curling interlocking twigs, swathed in an eerie, menacing fog. I saw towering tree trunks and an oppressively smothering canopy. I quivered at the edge of the forest of systems change work, unable to force myself to step in. I looked backwards and forwards, unsure of which way to turn. It was some time before I realised that the forest was not a place to fear, but an enlightening and enchanting world of compassion and love to be embraced.

What do you mean, you 'love us'?

Six months earlier, I had been in a rather large and busy conference hall in a grand old building in the centre of London. You know the type. It was one of those rooms where everything echoes because the room is so large. Round tables spanned so far that you could barely see who was on the other side of the room. Water jugs clinked, microphones whistled, and everyone was leaning forwards slightly, straining to hear the speaker.

It was mainly people from public services in the room. In the middle of a talk, the black shiny microphone started to do the rounds, being passed from one person to another, one table to another. A few crackles and high-pitched squeaks later and a tall, middle-aged woman from the NHS stood up and said to a group of people sitting two tables away, 'Look, we don't want to fight with your team, we love you

29

all.' Her voice almost cracked as she said it. Her quivering vocals were a clear sign of the emotion, honesty and bravery it took to stand up in front of 100+ people, take to the microphone and make such a statement. The room fell silent. There was a pause. People glanced from side to side at each other, not knowing how to respond. Then, a long and honest conversation took place between the two tables, in view of the whole conference room about how they all wanted to stop the fighting, stop competing, stop the desperate need to be seen to be best and bring some humanity back into their working relationships once again.

The word love took me by surprise. I was not used to hearing that word in this kind of context. It felt uncomfortable for me, like a small snake wriggling around in my tummy, making me feel nauseous. I could feel myself gently frowning, my lips pursing together and my chin and forehead crinkling at the discomfort.

About one month later, I was running a systems thinking workshop with another group of people from the NHS, and it came up again. This strange and intriguing word that gave me feelings of discomfort. 'We love each other in this group'. The wriggling in my tummy started again, as I considered what it was I was really hearing. An expression of true love? Or something else? Of course, I then had to go off on an adventure of reading and talking to people to discover what I thought people meant and why the word love was becoming predominant in conversations about work. It was on this curious journey that I came across the book, *Love 2.0. How our supreme emotion affects everything we feel, think, do and become*, by Barbara L. Fredrickson.

One quote in the book by Margaret Atwood struck me: 'The Eskimos had fifty-two names for snow because it was important to them: there ought to be as many for love'. Maybe there should be. I became aware that I had been defaulting to thinking that love was one particular thing, a romantic relationship, even though I had used the word to define a good working relationship in the past. I became aware that even though my use of the word love was wide and varied, I still defaulted to thinking about romantic love when I heard the word used by others. It made me consider just how deeply set our perceptions are and how we project those outward. The wriggling snake in my tummy was the perfect example.

Digging deeper into the topic area, I was blown away to discover that love can occur with even the smallest encounter. This idea gave me permission and a completely new framing with which to see, understand and experience the expression of the word love. It took me back to when I had first read Humberto Maturana's Book, *The Origins of Humanness in the Biology of Love*. It was this book that encouraged me to consider the underlying emotions in our situations and how they might impact people's work and how they interact with others. I wondered where and when we had lost the emotion of love from our working lives.

In the challenging times that were upon us all, locked down in our homes, I wondered if we were hungering for oneness and love. For connection. For mutual care. I suspected so. The wriggling subsided, the snake dissolved, and I felt calm again.

Social creatures

This encounter with the word love reminded me of the craving for social inclusion, belonging, nurturing, and relationships that we all have, which has become another central concept in my systems practice. I read about this in Matthew D. Lieberman's book, *Social. Why our brains are wired to connect* in 2013 and immediately embedded my learning from the book into the way I practised. I focused on values, beliefs and identity, and the human craving to be socially connected.

Matthew Lieberman explains that we can experience damage to our social bonds in the same way we experience pain. It's interesting, isn't it? That we are so sensitive to social rejection.

I guess, being wired to be part of a gang, to have connections and to belong can be a good thing. But if that sense of belonging in an organisation or workplace is dependent upon keeping our heads down, keeping quiet about issues and not doing anything radical, people are likely to conform to this norm. They need the belonging, and they need the work.

Some say it is useful to challenge conformity and encourage ourselves and others to stick our heads above the parapet and make bold or different moves. Take chances. Be risk-takers and dare to fail. But what about the fear of social rejection as a result of standing out? Do we know the extent of what we are asking people to step into? Do we encourage people to equip themselves to deal with the pain of exclusion? How do we support them as they reduce their fear, so that it becomes manageable? Do we need to? How do we create an environment together that allows people's authenticity to flourish, showcasing their gifts, their personality, their talents, their plethora of ideas, their powers of connection and excellent networking abilities? How do we support and encourage each other as we forge collaborative partnerships?

Hidden gems

This fear of rejection can lead people to become a shadow form of themselves. Often, people adopt a persona to fit in and avoid the pain of social exclusion. I know many people, whom I would consider system thinkers, who would like to speak out and challenge the norms in their workplaces and society. I observe them remaining hidden like precious gems embedded in a dull rock face. They are unrecognised diamonds. The jewels remain hidden with heavy hearts, shrouded in the identity of an imposing, grey organisation. Fitting in is their way of avoiding the pain of social exclusion or even worse, dismissal and loss of their job or even their career. They avoid the pain but pay the price with a lack of fulfilment. It is written in every deeply carved wrinkle of their faces. Their true values fall like discarded leaves in a cool autumn wind because they are at odds with the values of the organisation and/ or society they serve. Joy and fulfilment are soon replaced by monotony and regime.

It sometimes seems impossible to move forward from this place. Maintaining the belief that it is possible is crucial. If we do not have hope, what do we have? We can build relationships, alliances, reciprocal supportive networks and communities. We can nurture and motivate each other. We can cooperate and form partnerships. We can encourage the beautiful gems to have the courage to pop out from the grey wall and dance and shine in all their vibrant, glorious beauty. We can help each other to believe in ourselves. That is what I aim for in my systems practice when I undertake systems change work. I help others to evolve these supporting conditions and celebrate the people who encourage themselves to truly shine, like the brightest twinkling stars in an inky black sky.

Power struggles

Of course, there is always a danger that others do not want the gleaming gems to shine. They do not want to create the conditions of nurturing, sharing, and encouraging individuals to exercise their gifts to the full. They prefer power and control. They like to keep people in their place so that their own world does not get rocked.

Power and control are the strongest barriers to using systems thinking that I have come across. They seek to stamp out the nurturing enablers that encourage people to think freely and openly, share and discuss, listen and understand. This is particularly true of power cliques, who merge and become large toxic hives of manipulation, creating a self-serving feedback loop that keeps them continually nourished with delicious toxicity. These are the ones who can find the true enablers of change unpalatable because it takes away their power, dilutes their control and encourages people around them to peep their heads out from behind the obscuring hierarchy to show off their magnificent talents.

Those clinging to power and control tend to like the idea of using systems thinking to make change, but only if they are the only ones to 'do it'. This goes completely against the ethos of systems thinking, which is and should be accessible to all. We can all fall for being like this at times. We are part of a world where power and control predominate, and it is easy to get sucked in. It is built into the very way that society moulds us, the way we are taught and the way we are subtly encouraged to live our lives. Sometimes, you need to stop and ask whether you are the one protecting a power base. Are you controlling others? Are you preventing those around you from shining brighter? If so, it is never too late to change.

I have now engaged with many people craving to bring humanity back into their work situations. I have conversed with many people eager to harness and utilize their own creativity and I hope I am starting to see the ripples of change.

Dancing in the enchanted forest

Nowadays in my work, I sometimes feel as I did when I discovered the book, *A Simpler Way* by Margaret Wheatley and Myron Kellner-Rogers. When I read it, I felt like I was standing beneath a refreshingly cool waterfall of positivity. Only seventeen pages into the book and I was awash with words like belief, optimistic, creative, purposeful, explore, diverse and identity. I felt inspired, eager to read on. In one sense, I felt they were stating the obvious. That which is inside us all is desperate to come out and play. Our desire to explore, discover and create, to belong and have meaning in our lives that supports our identity; an identity that we choose, rather than one that is imposed upon us.

I was reminded that the universe is alive and constantly changing. It organises and creates identity. Think about that for a moment. Consider its relevance in terms of your workplace and your job. What could it mean for the identity of the teams and groups you are part of? How many opportunities do team members have to be creative in line with their own identity and what impact does that have on them? Does it impact their belief in themselves? And on their belief in the group as a whole?

This was something that hit me between the eyes and ever since I have considered the notion of identity in my work. What does it mean for groups of people like social workers, who want to give the best support to the people they help and yet austerity cuts mean that they cannot? What does it mean for support workers who strive to support people in securing safe accommodation and the basic comforts of life who are thwarted by bureaucracy and policies that work against them? It is any wonder that they can end up in a state of crisis themselves because of constantly coming up against brick walls that stand in the way of what they want to do and how they want to do it? Consistently having to enact your job in a way that you do not agree with can have a significant impact on your identity and that, in turn, can crush who you believe you are as a person. Identity is a small word, but it is certainly no small thing.

Is this 'the way' then?

Am I saying that this is THE way we should always approach things when we want to enable systems change? With compassion and empathy, considering things like identity and love? Not always. It is one way that has been relevant in my systems practice journey in recent years, but these things are not an easy area of exploration for a lot of people. Everyone is in a different place with their life journey. With how comfortable they are with others. With exploring their identity, knowing their purposes and being ready to engage with these concepts. My systems practice always has two elements - exploration of the situation, and exploration of ourselves. What I have come to realise over time is 'exploration of ourselves' can be a challenge for many people.

But how did I get here? To this very point of using my systems practice, with a sense of humanity and love, to support those creating systems change? This was definitely not the journey I set out on, and it was certainly not the journey I imagined in any way, at any time, in my past. Exploring and working with systems thinking and embodying it in your own systems practice is surprising like that. You start anywhere and it can take you everywhere. Let's see where I started and how this journey unfolded.

Chapter 2: Where it started

Spatulas and smurfs

'If you slam that bin one more time, I'm going to wrap this spatula around your neck!' she threatened gently with a death stare in her squinting eyes, metal spatula grasped in her fist, held just in front of his nose. Oh dear, here we go again.

'Erm, It wasn't my fault you left your measuring cylinders and beakers in the sink unwashed, again!' he responded defiantly, spatula raised as if ready for battle.

The laboratory I was in was a clean room with filtered air and controlled temperatures and air pressures. We wore full personal protective equipment all day. Yes, that means one of those awful masks we all had to wear during the pandemic and sometimes a full respiratory hood. We donned head-to-toe blue gowns, white lab shoes and latex gloves. On top of that, we had white mesh mob caps to keep our hair covered and white plastic aprons. We looked like some weird hallucinogenic version of *The Smurfs*.

The twelve labs of varying sizes had no windows to the outside world. They had white shiny walls that we could easily wash down every week, black vinyl floors that required daily hoovering and mopping before work could start and large white square ceiling tiles that were part of a monthly cleaning regime. Despite the oppressive surroundings we were all good friends and usually in good humour. 'The family' we called ourselves. That is not a phrase I would use nowadays, but it was apt at the time. The gentle threats about spatulas being wrapped around each other's necks were quite normal and done in jest. Although on that occasion, I had to draw an imaginary line down the middle of the floor to keep the two warring parties apart. All in good spirits, of course, and it became our story about the fun we had that day for some time afterwards.

Working in a pharmaceutical 'specials' lab was just the best. We made bespoke medicines by hand. Lollipop, lozenge, ointment, elixir or suppository anyone? A suspension maybe? How about some pastilles? I learnt things like what flavourings NOT to mix with quinine sulphate. Some make your mixture bubble up, expand and resemble the magic porridge pot, which just keeps bubbling over, bubbling over, bubbling over.

I remember with great fondness the day I accidentally set a Hobart mixer on full speed with over 20kg of warm liquid paraffin and white soft paraffin in the bowl. For those non-pharmaceutical people out there, think giant food mixer with 20kg of heated, molten Vaseline in it mixed with warm greasy liquid paraffin. Think not putting the mixer arm down far enough and not noticing. Think hitting the fastest mix speed, instead of the slowest. Yes, that! And think of me and the guy I was working with ending up looking like two giant candles, covered in molten gloop. Then came the four-hour room clean-up! But I tell you, I still laugh out loud about it today. Thank you, John, for helping me to clean the room. You were such a pal.

It is not just the fun that I want to share with you. These were the formative years of my systems thinking mindset and subsequent practice, which were developing without my conscious knowledge at the time. More and more, I realise the value that every past job has brought to my current systems practice. I started my working life as a Registered Pharmacy Technician. It was not my intended career path. I kind of fell into it, being dazed and confused when I left the school system. But I can say that it taught me some valuable skills that I carry with me today.

The human error investigator

So how did my days in the labs give me a solid grounding for my systems practice? I became heavily involved in improvement, quality and training. Improving our processes and procedures came easily to me and yet things still went wrong sometimes. This is where I realised the importance of the people involved in the processes. Not just whether they were trained, but whether they were comfortable and happy in their working environment.

As well as training in quality improvement, I learned how to reduce human errors. I became a human error investigator and auditor and it brought some of the most exciting insights about people into my world of work. It taught me how the colour of the walls could affect our mood. How the lighting could give us headaches and make us feel sluggish. How the layout of our working environments could help or hinder us and how people behaved as human beings. Until that point, I had not realised how much being human impacted us unconsciously. What we see or do not see. What happens when we are tired or unhappy. What we recall and what we can easily miss. It was a truly fascinating experience that revealed the importance of considering human factors and foibles when looking at work situations.

When I became a quality assurance auditor, I learnt what it meant to observe. I mean really observe. I looked at the labs, I looked at the work, I looked at the people. I observed body language, looking for signs of nervousness or discomfort. I watched how people moved around the labs, how they interacted with each other. I learnt how to listen and understand what people were really saying to me, rather than just hearing their words. As people told me how many orders they had completed that day, I was already reconciling it with what I could see on the schedule board behind them, how many orders were on their 'in trolley', what state the lab was in and how they were behaving as they talked to me. I could easily notice a shake of the hand and a change in the tone of the voice. I could spot a discrepancy in an instant. I looked for complete or incomplete batch records, weight tickets for each ingredient, records being correctly signed and dated. I looked for labels to say when equipment had been cleaned and whether it was within an acceptable timeframe. At the same time, I could spot dust on the back of a water pipe behind the sink without even turning my head. These observational skills were to become crucial in my future systems practice, yet at the time I had no idea how.

One in, all in

I did not carry out my observations alone. I worked alongside several other team leaders and supervisors in the laboratory environment. At the time, I gave little appreciation to how well we worked together. We actively coached each other every day. We had five to ten minute catch-ups in the morning, at lunchtime and midway through the afternoon. We checked we were all ok, that the work was going well and if not, we actively worked together to help the areas that were struggling.

All of the staff in the labs worked with the same ethos. If there was a crisis, it was 'one in, all in' and no one left behind. We were all very open and honest with each other and were not afraid to show our vulnerability. We supported each other peer to peer, and we were left to get on with it by our senior manager, who allowed us the autonomy to make effective decisions. We had access to any information we required and fast mechanisms to raise issues, should any arise. People were approachable, helpful and willing to pull together if needed. We considered the feelings of those in our labs as much as we could. We were not focused on hierarchy but on being decent human beings. We even practised one Tai Chi move together in our team meeting every morning. I still have contact with some of those friends to this day.

There was not always 'one best way' to do our work but we did have strict protocols for some elements. We worked to Good Manufacturing Practice guidelines and were inspected by the Medicines and Healthcare Products Regulatory Agency. There were things we were obliged to do to maintain the quality of the medicines we made. After all, one slip on our behalf, an incorrect medicine dosage, could mean a dead person 24 hours later.

Yet there was scope for flexibility around how we managed our workload and how we worked together in the labs. How we reduced fatigue. How we developed our rotas to maintain skills and avoid boredom. How we remained sane, locked together in our clean rooms, day after day with little contact with the outside world. We were our authentic selves with each other and reciprocated readily. Deals were made. You help our lab to make this cade oil ointment on time (it stinks like rotting fish) - we help you clean your lab tomorrow at 6 am. We formed relationships within teams and between different teams. We had agreements about what we would do if one lab hit difficulties part-way through the day. We had an up-front reciprocal arrangement in place to share staff and prioritise together. We were flexible and pulled together when it mattered.

We reviewed our progress as individuals and as a team, and took corrective and preventative actions for anything consistently going wrong. We learnt from each other's mistakes. (I repeat, do not put the wrong flavouring into a quinine sulphate mixture!) News spread quickly so that the next lot of people on the rotation did not do the same thing. We shared openly and had effective handovers when we moved between labs. We talked about what worked and what didn't during these handovers. We discussed formulas we had tried and what to steer clear of. At the time, I did not realise that we were developing and manipulating powerful feedback loops and mechanisms of coordination. This resonated when much later, I discovered that a core element of something called a Viable System Model (VSM) is coordination. If you have not heard of the VSM before, read on. You will find out more about it a little further on.

In the lab, the feelings of power and control were quite minimal, and people were happy to be accountable for their actions and decisions. We did not just monitor our failure rates, although we did that regularly. We looked at how we were operating together. We experimented with break times, with different rotations. We explored how we could flex quickly, moving from small one-off item manufacturing to batch manufacturing and back again, until we got the balance right.

A changing world

What the organisation was not so good at, was appropriately understanding the impact of changes in our environment. Rules changed, and community pharmacists were no longer allowed to make one-off bespoke manufactured prescription items in the dispensary of their retail pharmacy stores. They had to order from organisations like ours, who had fully quality-compliant premises and staff, to reduce the chance of errors. Our orders skyrocketed. We opened new labs, batched things together, trained staff to do more, recruited more staff, put on extra shifts and worked seven days a week, all in an attempt to amplify our internal variety, increasing our ability to deal with demand. We were too slow though. We became swamped with orders and could not keep up. Looking back, I see that the organisation had not been quite quick enough to bring in information about the outside environment. I later discovered this is what Stafford Beer, an expert in the science of managing organisations, describes as the intelligence function (System 4) in his VSM.

When information did come into the organisation, we responded with an increase in lab space and staff capacity to deal with it as quickly as possible but, alas, we were too slow and we disappeared into the quicksand, our exhausted mouths gulping for air as we were taken over. The operations moved to the other side of the country and the premises we had come to love, closed. We had worked so hard, and it was a very sad time.

I remembered with fondness our squabbles, our stand-offs with spatulas at twenty paces. I remembered our Children in Need day when we learned that you can indeed turn into characters from children's television programmes when dressed in full personal protective equipment. My dear friend Alice, a fun yet fierce Geordie, drew a giant women's chest on her apron. Instead of calling herself Crystal Tips from the children's programme Crystal Tips and Alistair, she christened herself Crystal T*ts! It would not have been so funny had we not committed to answering the phone that day with our cartoon name. I do not think I have laughed so much in my life. Alice eventually moved to Cyprus with her husband, after the organisation closed down. A few years later, I said my goodbyes to her over the phone as she parted this world. We talked about our days in the labs and what fun we had. That phone call was one of the hardest things I have ever had to do in my life, and I will never forget you, Crystal T*ts.

Into the unknown

It was a turbulent work journey thereafter, for a few years. I entered the world of the NHS to do a medicines management project and I can tell you that the culture shock was nothing less painful than being dipped head-first into a barrel of icy water. The strangulating bureaucracy and power structures crushed my chest, taking my breath away. The lack of autonomy was like I had been frozen into an ice cube and the pace felt so slow it had the potential to put a snail to sleep. No one shared anything. There were few repositories of information. Those that did exist were next to useless. You were treated like you were in school, having to get even the most basic of letters or pieces of work checked by a senior manager. I was desperately unhappy with this new world and longed for my days in the frantic yet invigorating laboratory with my fast-paced work and interesting friends again.

Yet there is always a way to continue the type of work that you love, and I did have a certain degree of autonomy. I worked on a project to incorporate pharmacy staff into an Intermediate Care team. These teams consisted of nurses, social workers, therapists and support workers, and they supported older people when they came home from hospital and still had health or care needs. The project aimed to help older people take their medicines appropriately upon leaving hospital and I put my skills to the test in a new environment.

The go-between

I soon put my observation skills to work. I sought out the issues with pathways and communication, protocols and relationships. I got used to working in a multi-agency fashion and made a whole raft of new friends. The project started with a focus on process mapping and quality improvement. While I did not realise it at the time, I was naturally drawn to supporting activities and considering how governance supported or hindered the work. This was back in 2004.

I targeted areas where I could create communication networks and build relationships between stakeholders. I went out and visited community pharmacies from across the whole patch and informed them of our project. I got them interested and, in some cases, involved.

I met with whole pharmacy groups to gather their perspectives about how we could help older people take their medicines as prescribed. I met with joint care management teams, made up of social workers and nurses, and I met with home care teams to ask them what they could bring to the project. I shadowed joint care managers and home carers, picking up on the things that a conversation could never tell me. I observed how they felt and acted. I noticed points at which they became anxious as time pressures came down on them like a heavy weight. Times when I could clearly see the joy they got from helping the people they cared for. I did morning shifts, evening shifts, and daytime shifts and I can tell you that it was exhausting. I met with the primary care trust pharmacists and brought in their perspectives, and they contributed by training care home staff in how to manage medicines better.

I acted as the go-between. The relationship builder. The observer. The modeller. I created channels of communication and supported others as they developed as a network of people all pulling in the same direction. I looked at the processes involved from several perspectives. I considered whether different stakeholders recognised and understood each other's needs. I looked at whether they could manage each other's expectations and whether they shared any areas of commonality in their visions and goals. I looked at the availability of resources, structures and logistics, and the environment. I explored the culture of the organisations and the people involved. I exposed problems and areas of weakness. I read policies, written procedures, and laws. I observed actual procedures, which were, of course, nearly always different to what was written down. I considered processes and how they might continually improve, a perspective I had brought forward from my days as a quality auditor. I explored the professions of the people, their backgrounds and their training. I looked at their paperwork and how it was used. I delved into supporting systems like I.T. I observed how people behaved together and how relationships were working.

The small things

I went out to GP practices and found they were keen to be an active and supportive player and, of course, I visited patients. I sat with them in their homes. Held their hands as they talked to me about their families. I watched as they battled to open tablet packages, as they struggled when they realised that all their medicines had fallen out of the packets into the bottom of a plastic bag at 5 pm on a Friday night and there was no one to help them sort it out. Having had a disabled parent, I knew about the small things to help them cope in the moment.

I remember one older woman who was quite distressed because her failing eyesight meant that the two tablet boxes in front of her seemed identical. One lot of tablets was to be taken once a day and the other twice. She could not tell which was which. You may be familiar with blister packs, the plastic boxes with compartments for each day of the week to separate medicines. This was before they were widely used, so we needed to think of something else. Off I trotted to the local pharmacy and bought a packet of hair ties, the type that consisted of a rubber band with two coloured balls attached to the band. I tied one around the packet that was to be taken twice a day and with the other one, I cut off one of the balls, so it was left with only one ball on the elastic band and tied that around the box that was to be taken once a day. It was a temporary measure until we could think of something better, but I cannot explain the joy I felt as I saw the stress dissolve away from the face of a lonely woman. I informed the local pharmacy of what I had done, and they picked up working with her to think of a longer-term solution. Communicating that message to others who were caring for her was key. I put a lot of effort into doing it. I realised that most of what I was doing involved developing ways of communicating quickly and effectively, but that was built on the relationships I had nurtured with those people and the meaning of the project that I and others had made together.

Returning home

Despite the moments of joy I felt when exploring something new, I bounced back out of medicines management as quickly as I had entered it. I felt bored and stifled like I had hurtled backwards by many years at an amazingly fast speed. I entered the world of production management in clinical trials. I worked for an organisation that needed to adhere to Good Manufacturing Practice for the first time and away I went. I found it easy, invigorating, exciting and stimulating. I worked with full autonomy again as production manager and the days flew. The quality of my work was highly praised by the inspiring medical director, and I felt like I was home again.

The only thing I did not like was that clinical trials do not respect weekends or holidays. Days and nights blurred into one with dosing regimes at 8 am and 8 pm. Whilst I loved the work, I felt like a prisoner to it. One evening I sat in my office watching the mature trees outside swaying in the gentle wind. It was a dark and quiet yet strangely comforting autumn night. I had been on site since 6 am due to having to oversee the assembly of a batch of injections for dosing that morning and because new clients needed to meet the production manager in person. They had gone to dinner. I was supposed to be there too, but it was 8 pm and I was exhausted. All I wanted to do was to go home. I was mesmerised by the swaying of the trees outside of the window for around an hour. Suddenly, I glanced up and saw my reflection in the darkened window. How had I become so tired? My eyes had jet black bags underneath. My skin looked pale and lifeless. I was trembling slightly, and I was beyond tired. I knew that although it was now 9 pm, I would have to be back again, at 6 am to oversee the preparation of the lab and the drugs, ready for dosing at 8 am. It was an excellent job. A high position. Very good wages. An excellent package of additional benefits, including things like private health care. I was learning so much every day. I was intellectually stimulated but my body was tired. I stared back at my reflection and whilst I loved the nature of the job, I knew something had to change or I would grind myself into the floor by my late 30s.

I also missed studying. I had put a business degree on hold because I could not manage it alongside my very long working hours. This did not feel good to me. I had always studied academically alongside my work. I was unable to go to university after school because of personal circumstances, so once I started earning money, night school it was. I studied pharmaceutical science, management, quality management, operational management, human resource management, strategic management, and techniques like Six Sigma and Lean, and I was now on the lookout for something else. The management degree I started but did not finish was ok, but I had soon become bored, studying things I had already been putting into practice for a long time.

I looked around for something different. Something that would bring together elements of improvement, managing effectively, engaging with situations, and of course, was focused on people. I had previously been under the illusion that human resources was about people. By the time I came to the end of an HNC in Business and Human Resource Management at Teesside University, I was very clear that it was not. I gained a distinction in the course and won the Ede and Ravenscroft prize for excellence on the programme, but I could not see myself doing it long-term.

I searched and searched until I discovered something called systems thinking. There were several undergraduate courses available at the Open University. The minute I saw the content, I knew it was what I wanted to do and off on a new adventure I went, with my laptop and internet connection at the ready and a whole new style of learning to engage with. It was terrifying thinking about learning in a completely different way from being in a classroom with people. I had no idea how I would take to it, but I was desperate for further intellectual stimulation and so I signed up. Little did I know where the journey would take me.

Getting on with the real work

Not long after, I moved into NHS commissioning. It was urgent care commissioning so it felt fast-paced, a little frantic and full of interesting organisations and characters. Compared to my previous job, I was paid less, there were fewer perks, and it was lower status, but I got good paid holidays and bank holidays off. I could work 8 am to 4 pm and know that I would finish work on time. I could also undertake my qualifications alongside work quite easily. While I had more autonomy than in medicines management, bureaucracy, control, power cliques and unwritten and underhand rules of the game predominated.

Thankfully, a wise older woman from a local authority, with years of public service experience took me under her wing. In those early days, she told me: 'Don't worry kid, I'll show you how to deal with this bloody lot. Especially those on their power trips. I'll show you how we deal with them and make them leave us alone so we can get on with the real work.' And she did. She soon became, and still is, a very close friend. We have our regular lunch dates, and our friendship deepens by the month.

At first glance, commissioning seemed a logical approach to improving health outcomes. Yet the turbulent journey through multiple disciplines and across organisational interfaces rarely made it an easy job. So, I welcomed with open arms the System Dynamics from my Open University course which allowed me to model and understand the complex areas of hospital discharge and urgent care. It supported me to examine the potential consequences of different configurations of processes and their dynamics, vastly informing my commissioning decisions.

Making a difference

I can tell you this, no matter how bad a problem seemed at first glance, it rarely needed a huge commissioning exercise to make at least some kind of improvements. It just required a different perspective and an understanding of how things worked in context.

Figuring out where to start in such a complex landscape, however, could be overwhelming. The systems approaches I was learning about gave me entry points. Stafford Beer's VSM for example taught me how to explore organisational arrangements and governance and how to spot variety imbalances that were preventing processes and departments from operating to their maximum effect.

More often than not, several strategic tweaks, informed by rigorous examination of working practices, structures and dynamics, were all it took to make a difference. By difference, I mean maintaining delayed discharge figures at below national and regional average for over three years, gaining sign-up from three major regional hospitals to a Transfer of Care Protocol, understanding and preventing the reasons for high care home admissions to hospitals, building effective and efficient escalation systems that people actually responded to, reducing frequent callers to the ambulance service, to name but a few. I must add, though, that these improvements were made at a time before the extended years of austerity cuts that give us our current challenges. Even the very best of systems thinking struggles to deal with those.

In the early days, the key thing that my systems practice taught me was that examining the thinking behind decision-making was essential. This enabled me to engage with and improve on the multi-organisational relationships that were so prevalent in commissioning. I first needed to understand the common patterns of thinking in each of the stakeholder groups so that I could highlight areas of joint understanding and areas of difference and the implications. This proved beneficial as I embarked on Easter planning, winter planning, and emergency planning, and inputted heavily to an urgent care stakeholder management group.

I highlighted issues that had not been openly raised before. Things like how to avoid one organisation or person from taking an individual stance to the detriment of others. How to support and encourage a non-threatening interface between different players. Where responsibility, accountability and authority lay and whether it was helping or hindering the collective. The perverse impact of our confrontational performance management and how we might consider different forms of monitoring.

Touching a nerve

I found the combination of complex multi-agency operations and strategic commissioning both satisfying and stimulating. I introduced systems concepts, such as emergence and systemic inquiry to my colleagues, although that did not go as planned. One time, one of the directors we worked with demanded a report about why it was beneficial to develop a network of stakeholders who could quickly act together to resolve urgent care issues. The NHS loves reports, and I had my orders, so a report it was.

'What on earth is this? I don't understand any of it!' His voice boomed and he was pretty red in the face. I had slipped some systems thinking language into it, in the hope of stimulating some curiosity and/ or debate. The words systemic inquiry had got him. It had clearly not been understood and had touched a nerve. To say the director hated it, or the feeling it gave him, was an understatement.

Or so I thought. At the time I was not wise enough to realise this was a multi-agency director's meeting for me to present my report, and it was also a political game. At the director level, I observed them pulling apart, determined to go in their separate directions to meet their own crushing demands and performance metrics. I knew that change was most powerful when it came from multiple levels, so I was determined to keep the directors on board with the approach that everyone below them in the hierarchy knew was right. At the end of the meeting, I took the report away and rewrote it, as I had been instructed to do. Well, I say I rewrote it. I changed only a handful of words and presented it back to them. Yes, the words I changed were 'systemic inquiry'.

It was a tense meeting, but I argued my corner. I went head-to-head with the director from a partner organisation. He was trying to wriggle away into his burrow, but I was having none of it, highlighting what I felt was right. Our relationships were key and if we did not foster them, grow them, and make meaning of the complexity in front of us together then we would all suffer. It was a legendary debate, so I am told. It did not feel like it at the time. It just felt stressful and difficult. Apparently, I remained calm throughout. During a break, the same director approached me in the corridor. He came right up to my face, only inches away, invading my private space. He pointed straight at me, at the level of my nose. I thought, 'Here we go again!' Now face to face, he quietly said to me, loud enough for me to hear but not others, 'I like you! I bet your organisation has no idea what to do with you or how to use you!'

We returned from our break for what I thought was going to be round two. I tentatively took my seat and waited. Every recommendation in the report remained the same as in my first presentation. 'Wonderful! Absolutely wonderful, Pauline! See what happens when you listen to us and do as we say. This is much, much better.' They endorsed my report and every suggested action in it. I remained quiet and had a gentle giggle to myself as I left the room. Right up until 2021, I was repeatedly asked, by people I had not worked with for many years if I still had the System Dynamics diagrams that I included in that report and if they could please have a copy.

After that meeting, every Friday at 7 am, my phone would ring. (Yes, I started work at 7 am on Friday because it was always a Friday when things kicked off in urgent care.) Dead on 7 am, before anyone else was in the office. Ring, ring! Ring, ring! It was the very same director from the partner organisation asking me if everything was going ok, did I need him to do anything for me and if there was anything he should know about or should be doing something about. The lesson I learnt – people do not like being called out face-to-face or being made to feel like they do not understand something and will often react badly to it. They do often want your help though. They just do not want everyone else to see them asking for that help or you giving that help. It is a lesson I have held with me and the learning from it still stands today. I was happy to oblige and help him in private. We worked effectively together, below the radar, every week, for years afterwards. Up until now, I barely told a soul.

A call for help

Word must have got out about my 7 am start on a Friday. One Friday my phone rang a little earlier than normal. Luckily, I had arrived early with my coffee and bagel in hand. When I picked up it was not the director I had expected but the chief executive of a hospital in a neighbouring region. They had a particularly tricky situation to deal with relating to the reconfiguration of their hospital sites. It was Friday morning and they needed help.

'Only you really know how your area might help us the best. Please help us. What can you do?' I did help, and to maintain the anonymity of the hospital and chief executive I will not go into too many details. However, I can say that as a network, we pulled together and placated what could have been quite a tricky situation for emergency departments that weekend. We drew on up-front reciprocal agreements around collaboration and support to get through. Thankfully, the weekend went by without issue.

I did not do everything though. All I did was pull the strings of the spider's web that we had created together. We had obliterated false calls for help earlier, so everyone knew that when our network asked for help it was a genuine request. They all responded accordingly and admirably. I was later asked to become involved in emergency planning across our region and the neighbouring region thereafter.

I welcomed systems thinking approaches with open arms as I engaged with this new and enticing world of work. They helped me to encourage meaningful conversations across multiple boundaries, with an understanding of the different reference systems at play. It is all too easy in those situations to forget that many problems are rooted in the complex, messy structures of which we are a part. We slip into incorrectly apportioning blame to people for anything seen to be going wrong. The danger, of course, is inappropriate commissioning decisions with ineffective outcomes, potentially creating a system that is even harder to navigate.

Unbeknown to me at the time, the methods, concepts, tools and techniques that I was learning back then were forming a solid bedrock that I would use to examine and navigate complex, dynamic and diverse problematic situations. A sophisticated commissioning approach, incorporating systems thinking, had proven to me, time and time again, to be powerful, effective and believe it or not, quick. It was fast because I could see patterns rapidly. I could observe more effectively. I could react quicker. I could gain buy-in quicker. I could mobilise relationships quicker. I did not waste time doing the same ineffective things repeatedly, expecting to get different results. I could look at things from different perspectives, which significantly opened my range of opportunities for improvement.

Bringing additional benefits

Over time, I became increasingly aware of the benefits of systems thinking. My roles often involved working across more than one programme at the same time. My developing systems practice helped me engage with multiple programmes effectively and concurrently. My productivity increased, as I could engage with and understand large, complex situations much more quickly than before.

A combination of systems thinking, NHS commissioning, and my good friend who was guiding me through 'the way to deal with this bloody lot' helped me learn vital lessons. Here are the ones that still inform my practice today:

Lesson 1: People need a safe space and an opportunity to react, come to terms with, and articulate their feelings when change is being suggested or made

The director from the partner organisation taught me this. I became acutely aware that senior managers are expected by their peers and employers to know what to do. To admit not knowing was generally a sign of weakness and a lack of ability to do the job. What a shame that this mindset did and still does predominate in many organisations. In complex situations, you cannot possibly know all the answers or hold all the information about everything in your head. To expect you to do so is nothing but a way of setting you up to fail.

People need time and space to explore. They may need time to share thoughts and feelings. To articulate concerns and make suggestions. Challenging discussions will occur but that does not mean that it is all bad. I have since brought in techniques like clean language and non-violent communication to help with challenging discussions, facilitating a safe space for us to converse without conflict.

Lesson 2: It is useful to respect different views and perspectives

The systems thinking diagrams I used in my work, such as causal loop diagrams and rich pictures, allowed our perspectives and in some cases our feelings to be displayed without entering into a 'he said, she said' scenario. It dissolved previous tensions and made us see with a different lens. That which was previously unsaid started to rise to the surface and whilst we did not have all the answers, at least we could see what we were dealing with and start working with it.

Lesson 3: Allow time to accommodate conflicting interests and help people work through their understanding of the situation

This is a very underrated exercise. It is extremely valuable. In my experience, people hate feeling that their interest in a situation is not as valuable as someone else's. I helped people with this by engaging with and seeking to understand the complexity of the situation so that we gained a good understanding of each other's interests. Just knowing that the other parties understand your point of view can be a powerful tool to dissolve barriers.

Lesson 4: We can identify systemic issues in a situation, which can help us to consider what next steps might be possible if we want to make changes

Systems thinking has taught me to stay away from the blame game. This was particularly prevalent between health and social care at the time. Many times, people had nearly come to blows about things like the hospital discharge pathway. They blamed each other for failings instead of working together to resolve repeating patterns of issues. I used causal loop diagrams in particular to show the impacts of multiple causes and effects in our situation. This shifted the emphasis away from blame and onto how the dynamics in the scenario were causing vicious or virtuous feedback loops.

Lesson 5: There can be a lot of power in collective decision making

In commissioning, it was quite difficult to make decisions on our own, as one organisation. Our decisions impacted heavily on several other organisations we collaborated with and so making collective decisions about things became second nature. We learnt how to learn our way forward and make decisions together.

Appreciating the additional skills

These were just a small sample of the things that came to light for me at the time. I appreciated not only my early formative days of managing improvement and making change but also what systems thinking was bringing to the party for me personally. I went from being frightened of new complex situations, not knowing where to start, to seeing patterns of system behaviour and acknowledging people's boundary judgements. I got a sense of different perspectives quite quickly. I could see when people were falling into the traps of criticalness and blame. I could see where reinforcing feedback loops were occurring, resulting in vicious cycles, causing the situation to escalate out of control.

Systems thinking had minimised my fear. I had a deep sense of peace inside, no matter how big the challenge. Out of everything I had learnt and done to this point, that brought the most powerful benefits to my life.

And then came the Viable System Model in more detail

Over time, I became more fully acquainted with Stafford Beer's Viable System Model (VSM). For those who have not come across the VSM before, it was developed by Professor Stafford Beer, an international consultant in management sciences, who died in 2002. He was known for his work in operational research and management cybernetics. The VSM can be described as a way of looking at how we manage complexity in organisations or indeed, in anything we might perceive as a system.

I learnt from Beer's work that organisations, or systems, do not survive in a vacuum. They exist in a changing environment. Therefore, an organisation must be adaptive to the changing environment to survive (Beer, 1985). Unfortunately, the models we usually use to understand organisations generally only go as far as helping us understand the hierarchy or how a process works. There is little that helps us understand how the organisation manages complexity. This is what the VSM offers. A way of understanding how the organisation manages complexity and adapts to a changing environment.

The viable system monster

Initially, I found the academic texts about the VSM almost impenetrable and as such, it was not an easy introduction. There it was, in the corner of my change management party, staring at me like a drooling, growling, monster. But me being me, I could not resist poking it with a stick, just to see how it would react. It confused me, at first, because I was never quite sure if it was about an organisation or about organisation in general. This was mainly because the text I was learning from used both words so very closely together that I sometimes mixed the two up. I was not the only one either, several colleagues made the same mistake too. It was not long though before I realised it was about organisation, whether that was an organisation or any other kind of conceptual system, and we soon started to get along.

I was beginning to understand that two things were key for effective public services - managing complexity at the right place and adaptability. For this reason, the VSM became an ideal candidate for use in my work. I now viewed the world of public service organisations very differently from when I first started working in the NHS.

I looked more deeply to see what made them breathe, what made their heart beat, what conditions had to exist to enable them to survive, what made them sick and what made them enter the throes of death. I probed deeper, considering how different services and teams interacted with each other and with their environment and how the individuals behaved. I looked at what interdependencies existed or did not exist but should or could. I examined the drivers of internal and external complexity and whether they were absorbed, matched, batted away or simply ignored. I studied the energy levels in situations. Were people and processes energised or frantic? I wanted to get a sense of whether people were stressed, fearful or in despair. Were they calm and laid back with not a care in the world? I considered not just, 'What is this thing?' but 'What does it do?' and 'How does it behave?'

I grew to see the value of the VSM. It helped me to see if there were any variety imbalances driving disorder in the systems I was engaging with. I considered interactions between the operations and the external environment to see if there was a relevant and appropriate value exchange. I looked for imbalances between the autonomy teams required to innovate and the cohesion the organisation needed to maintain its chosen identity. It encouraged me to explore whether the rate of change was causing problems. I identified where it was too fast and people were doing things that no one wanted yet and where it was too slow and teams were continuing to do things that no one wanted anymore.

Going deeper

I was able to dive much deeper into complexity. I recognised when resource conflicts arose as a result of weak resource bargaining. I observed turf wars between clinical teams, indicative of issues in coordination, known as system 2 in the VSM. I identified common elements of purpose across different teams and contemplated what that meant for those working together. I became mindful of system pathologies, which are patterns of system behaviour that can cause issues in situations. I noticed when they played a part in reducing the effectiveness of organisations and teams.

I also saw a human element embedded deeply within the model and concepts I was engaging with, hidden behind the technical texts that talked about structure and dynamics. Over time, I realised that the principles on which the VSM worked could be applied to almost anything. It struck me that I could use the VSM in a way that changed the context of the model from management to leadership, and then to system leadership. This influenced the development of my own systems thinking approach called Creating the Conditions for Change, which you will meet in part 2 of this book.

By now, I appreciated how observing deeply and really understanding how things worked helped me figure out what improvements to suggest. Whilst commissioning was not always about putting things right per se, I still felt it necessary to understand the situations I was engaging with to the fullest of my ability. The lenses I brought into my work shone a bright light into the dark corners. At the same time, they illuminated areas of current sparkling brilliance that were being overlooked. I gained greater, more relevant, and more useful insights every day. The huge bonus, as I mentioned previously, was that I was no longer scared of complex situations. I was no longer frozen, not knowing where to start. I was building my own approach to using and embodying systems thinking, drawing on multiple established models, methods, and concepts. I liked how it was supporting me to do my job. I also liked that I carried the thinking into my private life. I have to say that it changed the whole way I was engaging with and understanding things around me. I gained a strong sense of what my life meant to me and what it could be as I moved forwards, as a result.

Chapter 3: It's murder on the dancefloor

Corridor confrontations

'Pauline, you better come down here. There's an argument in the corridor again.' It was mid-morning and everything was going smoothly that week. I had the telephone held up to my left ear. The sun was shining in through the wall-to-wall office windows. The plants on the wooden side table were looking decidedly healthy in the bright sunlight. We had just had coffee and as a team we were calm and studious, getting on with the morning's work.

In the NHS there are a lot of restructures and people tend to move around a lot. I was no exception, and I was now working in quality assurance. I loved the team and the organisation. I felt calm and nurtured and like I belonged. My manager was one of the best I have ever had. She was intelligent and level-headed and supported her team brilliantly.

'You better make it quick, Pauline,' said the woman on the end of the phone, with an increasing sense of urgency. 'They're really having a go at each other today'. I got up from my desk and went down the back stairs and into the laboratory area below. I donned my thick white lab coat in the entrance doorway. I could see them halfway down the corridor, face-to-face in the middle of their stubborn squabble.

'Ok chaps. How are you doing? What's up? Can I help you with anything?' Imagine two quite heavy-set men standing a few metres apart, neither of them budging on their argument. It was about a small package which had been received into a department and appropriately stored in a refrigerator there. Surprisingly, the package was unable to sprout legs and walk itself down the corridor to the required laboratory and that was what the argument was about. No one would take it down the corridor to the lab and no one would come from the lab to collect it. Sounds incredible, doesn't it? But let me tell you a little more before you make a judgement.

Three strikes and you're out

The organisation's operations were highly regulated. It had to adhere to Good Manufacturing Practice and a whole raft of other quality assurance rules and regulations. As such, many of the activities were supported by Standard Operating Procedures (SOPs). If you have not come across SOPs before, they are a set of instructions about how to do certain elements of the job. They have to be strictly adhered to or the quality of the products could be compromised. The organisation had a very strict, 'three strikes and you're out!' policy. If you did not adhere to the SOPs, your job was literally on the line. No one was exempt. It was fair enough, considering the importance of the product. They were deadly serious about being exceptional at what they did.

The package had been received in one department. The SOPs in that department told them how to receive the package and how to store it, which was in a walk-in temperature-controlled refrigerator. The member of staff from that department did exactly what he was supposed to do. Yet in the other laboratory, their SOP stated, 'You receive the package into the laboratory'. There was no mention of the exchange between departments and how it should be carried out to maintain the integrity of the product. There was also nothing about informing the laboratory that a package had arrived or about how the laboratory could check whether a package had arrived for them. The argument was because the laboratory had needed the package thirty minutes previously and did not know it was in the refrigerator in the other department, at the other end of the corridor.

'Why did someone not just call them up and let them know?' I can hear you scream. Well, because it was not in their SOP and the staff knew that if they did something that was not in the SOP they could be disciplined and it was, 'three strikes and you are out.' It put everyone in an awkward position, which was why they had called in a member of the quality team for a seemingly simple thing.

Decision-making and autonomy

Of course, it was easy to sort this out. The immediate issue was to get the package to the correct laboratory and we sorted that out straight away. Then, I went through the process to get both SOPs changed so that the exchange between departments was covered and made clear to all in the future. I was now not just thinking just in operational terms or quality terms, however, I was also thinking in systems thinking terms. What I observed was control of individual actions, to a degree that was so rigid it gave absolutely no autonomy for decision-making with actions that the SOPs did not cover.

I also witnessed a situation where the same department refused a package because it was not part of a pre-arranged delivery but a one-off delivery. They adhered to the SOPs, but the package was desperately required and had been returned to the sender. Guess which laboratory it was for? Yes, you guessed it, the same one that was involved in the other dispute. It was no wonder they were frustrated.

Getting the balance of autonomy right for those working in an organisation can be tricky. It can have huge consequences. In this instance, there was so much time wasted on repeated petty arguments that could have been easily resolved if people had felt empowered to take a different course of action. When decision-making is taken away from an individual, they can easily feel disempowered and as a result, they might either take actions that seem totally contrary to common sense or no action at all. This is exactly what they are conditioned to do.

Yet when the outcome is not good, we are prone to falling into the trap of blaming individuals. Hence the argument with the two warring sides blaming each other for the dilemma that day. Each side believed the other was just being awkward and that was not the case. They were trying very hard to highlight that there was a real issue that needed to be resolved. What I believed I was seeing, apart from the usual lack of information in a SOP and somewhat rocky operational relationships, was an inability to respond to variety. Something happened that was slightly outside of the norm and autonomy had been reduced to such a degree that there was no quick or flexible way to deal with it. Whilst a seemingly small thing, when it happens repeatedly, it can cause a constant drip, drip, drip of frustration and eventually people snap and blame each other.

Riding the bicycle downhill

Sometimes, in systems thinking, loosening up the control and giving a little autonomy can be the right thing to do. Yet it can often feel counterintuitive. It is quite normal to think that if things have the potential to go wrong then you need to dictate the process down to every last detail and/ or make the rules even stricter. In my opinion, what is required is an appropriate balance between the rules required to maintain the integrity of a product or process and enough autonomy to deal with any other complexity that you might encounter in the day-to-day operations of your job. Of course, a highly regulated environment does not lend itself to having a lot of autonomy but in other situations, it can work very effectively.

How I describe this in workshops is to imagine you are riding a bicycle. You come to a steep hill you need to go down. The surface is a bit gravelly and uneven, and there is a bump like a ramp, at the bottom that you have to manoeuvre. Such a hill existed in my childhood. It was between the local shop that sold the very best children's sweets, comics and toys, and my house. I manoeuvred that hill many times on my red Grifter bike that Santa brought.

It was not easy, and I saw many a child go over their handlebars when hitting the bump at the bottom. Now imagine that you are going quite fast on your bike down that hill. You are constantly moving the pedals at different speeds, according to whether you want to go faster or slower. You are moving the handlebars in response to every bit of uneven surface. You might even periodically brake to avoid going too fast. It is your constant decision-making about your movements that allows you to get to the bottom and over that precarious bump in one piece. Now, imagine that you are at the top again and you are going very fast. Imagine your pedals have been set so that you can only pedal at one very fast speed, and you cannot slow down. Now imagine that you are not allowed to move the handlebars in response to the uneven surface. You are only allowed to hold onto them but how they steer has been set to one direction only. You are not allowed to use your brakes. Do you think you would get to the bottom and over that bump safely? Every child that tried to go down that hill at one steady fast speed ended up over the handlebars. Every child who did not steer their bike very well ended up over the handlebars. The two men in the adjoining departments had gone over their handlebars that day and crashed headfirst into each other in the corridor.

This was a very small example, but this pattern occurs repeatedly in organisations. Being able to deal with the complexity you are faced with daily is a key consideration in the VSM. At its heart is the concept of variety, and in particular Ashby's law of requisite variety, which basically states that however much variety the environment throws at us, we need an equal amount of responses to deal with it. If not, we are left in a position of not managing the variety, which can cause us issues. This was the concept I considered when the department received the package. Were all of the tasks the department was required to do considered fully? Could they match the variety they had to deal with every day? I contemplated that maybe they could if they just considered autonomy and decision-making more carefully.

What struck me was how deskilled people must feel in this type of scenario. How demoralising it must be. Imagine that you are the one being blamed for being awkward or difficult. In my experience, it is rarely anyone being awkward or difficult. It is just a human being responding to not being able to deal with the wealth of complexity they need to deal with every day. The knock-on effect can be time-consuming and exhausting for all involved.

Rabbits in the headlights

That being said, I do not advocate for just giving people a lot of autonomy and letting them 'get on with it!' Particularly if they have not been used to working with a lot of autonomy before. What can happen in this scenario, is they become paralysed with indecision, unable to find an appropriate way forward. They have been conditioned to wait for someone else to tell them what to do. Working with people to build up their confidence and outlining boundaries of autonomy can be a good place to start. I find it useful to consider how decisions should be made. Who will be consulted, if anyone? What kinds of things should be taken into consideration before the decision is made? When should a decision be made immediately and when can it wait? What I often find in organisations is that people expect others to know how to make decisions. They rarely consider that others might not know how to make decisions. This stands for people at a low level in the hierarchy, right up to very senior managers, some of whom I have seen immobilised by indecision.

The chaos caused by indecision can be irritating at best, and crippling at worst. I saw this play out some years later when I was working with a team of social workers at a local authority. I was working with them as a business consultant undertaking a service review. The team I met were burnt out and despondent after years of austerity cuts. Many had been on long-term sick leave. They had returned to work but still clearly looked unwell. The team had recently had a change of management and had gone from a very hierarchically-minded, controlling micro-manager to one who suddenly gave a lot of autonomy and told the team to just get on with it . The team had not worked with as much autonomy before and did not know how to. They were frozen, like rabbits caught in the headlights. They were dazed and did not know what to do. As a result, they ended up spinning around and around, like a child's toy spinning top, achieving not very much at all.

All that autonomy did almost as much damage as completely constraining them. Giving too much autonomy without support initially can cause immobilising, disorientation and even more stress. As with many things in a working environment, it is about how things are done as much as what is done. How you support people to enable them to make decisions is an often overlooked yet important consideration. Giving autonomy without supporting people to understand what it means for them is no more helpful than throwing a small rubber ring to someone splashing around in the middle of the ocean, being circled by hungry sharks.

The impact of my formal systems thinking education

My formal education in systems thinking was embedding more deeply now and I was cultivating my observational skills every day. I could see situations with several different lenses at the same time. I noticed where complexity was not being managed, where the balance between the autonomy of the individual and maintaining the cohesion of the organisation was working or not working and where patterns of unhelpful system behaviour were emerging. I could see where the reward systems in the organisation, official or unofficial, were limiting innovation. I was starting to understand the concept of self-organisation and that things cannot be planned down to the very last detail.

The ideas of communication and information were very interesting to me, and I will talk about my journey with these concepts in my next chapter. I was struck by the power of the insights from my formal education and how they strengthened my practice. I drew upon my other management and transformation expertise to help me decide what next . I was, of course, mindful that I was an integral part of the complex situations I was observing and as such, I was bound to have blind spots that I knew nothing about. I wondered if I was unearthing one of those blind spots one day when we came up against an intriguing puzzle.

We noticed that we had an increase in recorded quality incidents between midnight and 2 am in one department. Now, these quality incidents were very minimal and should not have been logged as incidents, but I was intrigued. What was going on between midnight and 2 am? Something clearly was. I checked all of the data we had available. Staffing levels for the department looked fine. Levels of demand looked fine. There was no sickness in the department. Shift patterns looked fine. I could see nothing amiss on paper and I remained curious. The department themselves claimed staff shortages. They had recently gone through a series of Lean improvements, and I wondered if they were just perceiving a shortage of staff in response to some changes they did not like. There was only one thing for it, I decided, and off on another exploration I went.

The lights at night

I walked into the brightly lit department, through large double doors at one end of the room. I immediately saw mouths agape and wide eyes staring at me.

'What on earth are you doing here?' I was asked

'I've come to see what you have to contend with during the night.' I replied. It was about 11 pm on a weekday evening.

'How long are you staying?' they queried

'Oh, probably until about 3 am. You keep telling me about all of the work you have to do so I've come to see it for myself.'

'Good! That's amazing. You're the first person who has been to see us during the night before, come down here and I'll introduce everyone.'

They were a marvellous team and very welcoming. The whole site we worked on had good relationships and they treated me very well. They showed me around and told me about the work they did. They told me their work stories, and their personal stories and I thoroughly enjoyed being there with them. Then………it happened!

It was midnight and it was pitch black outside of the windows. The site was not in a built-up area and there was very little light from streetlights or nearby houses. We were alone, in the middle of a tree-lined very dark space. I saw two bright lights up ahead, outside of the windows in the despatch doors. It felt eerie, partly because it had gone deathly quiet inside the department. You could have heard a pin drop. Then two more lights, glaringly bright. Two more followed and then another two. They just kept coming. I could feel the tension in the department rise.

Here we go they said, and chaos broke out. People were running around all over the place, moving boxes, opening doors. They were hurriedly scuttling up and down corridors, with a look of pressing determination on their faces. Doors were opening and closing so quickly that I found it very difficult to keep up with what was happening. This went on for two hours and then……silence. There was another hour of much less frantic activity to pull the department into shape again and then nothing.

'What happens now?' I said.

'Nothing, that's us done', they replied.

The lights had been the organisation's own delivery vans arriving, all at the same time. They came from the organisation's other geographical sites. Each of those sites had gone through programmes of Lean improvements. Each site and department within those sites ran very well as a result of the programme of improvements. Yet each one had gone through that process alone, with much less thought about the interfaces and interdependencies and interconnectivity with the other sites and departments. As a result, all of the vans turned up at this department at around the same time. Refrigerated vans vied for position at the plug-in points. They struggled to turn around to leave the site because there were so many other vehicles in the way.

The staff struggled to receive so much product into the department all at once and I clearly saw how this chaotic scene has arisen. The department had always maintained they did not have enough staff. The resource planners maintained that there were enough staff to cover a whole night shift, according to their metrics. Well, there were, if the work came to them in a rational and organised manner. As each unit scheduled the despatch of its vans in isolation, they had been blind to the impact on the receiving department.

And no, for those two hours, there were not enough staff to deal with what came gushing at them. I saw it with a clear quality assurance lens. I saw it from a resource planning lens. I also saw it from a systems thinking lens, in terms of the inability to deal with the variety that was coming at them for the two hours from midnight to 2 am. There was a lack of consideration for the interconnectivity between different geographical units. It was clear as a bright summer's day and yet before that point in time, had been invisible to those doing the number crunching and planning.

To aid my learning, I considered how I would define different elements of what was happening in more technical systems thinking terms. At one end of the department was a large, very wide, double door that opened out onto the area where the vans parked. This despatch area was where staff received the goods entering the department. A small hatch area was being built there, as the area was being remodelled. Drivers would come to the hatch and the team would deal with them and then, if required, they would admit them to the department, so they could bring their goods into the correct storage areas in a controlled way.

Embedding systems concepts

I began considering whether the hatch was part of the transduction boundary . A device that registers that something has happened and makes a message meaningful. What was it in this scenario that told the people in the department that the drivers had arrived? That was the first issue. There was no bell or buzzer or any other means for the drivers to alert the team to their arrival. We could see them arrive, of course, by the lights coming up the road. But what happened when the team weren't watching? I asked them.

'Oh, we don't see them and they end up finding the way in themselves. We have to chase them and bring them back out.' Curious, I thought. The area was being remodelled which would resolve the issue. They obviously had not got round to fitting the buzzer yet, or as I was considering it in my head, part of the transduction boundary. In the meantime, the message that stock had arrived was entering the department in a very erratic way. It all sounds technical for a simple thing, but it helped me to embed the concepts into my mind and thereafter, they were available for recall with bigger, more important, issues. I learnt the lesson of considering the concept on a smaller scale first while I became comfortable with it, before applying it to more complex and pressing matters.

In the meantime, I have to say that I laughed out loud seeing the drivers' heads speedily bobbing alongside the corridor window. They were like scuttling little mice, wriggling their way in through the smallest of unseen cracks and then scampering to the stock drop-off area as fast as their legs would take them, sharply followed by the department staff (the cats) trying to catch them. Up and down the corridor they went.

This is a very small example, but it is an example of how the additional lens I was using was bringing more insights into the work. In this case, it enabled me to consider whether the despatch interface was a transduction boundary. It helped me see the importance of the message coming into the system that the drivers needed attention. I understood the situations in technical terms, not just, 'Oh, they didn't get to the driver quickly enough because they were busy doing something else and did not know they were there.'

On the ground observations

The despatch area remodel was soon completed and the message about the timing of the vans was absorbed by the other sites and departments and acted upon. Calm was restored. The moral of the story? Always go and have a look. Every metric linked to this story, for example, resource metrics, number of vans, staff sickness levels, etc. told us things were fine. Staff were in danger of being blamed for moaning. Stafford Beer talks about system 3* in his VSM (Beer 1981). This is a monitoring function. It exists to see if performance and other metrics are telling the truth about a situation. I knew to go and do a night shift because, in this scenario, we were missing this monitoring function and relying on metrics to tell us the story. Just look at how different the story was when we got some on the ground observations from a peer from a different department who could understand what they were seeing. The issues in the situation had not been fully recognised but now we had a much clearer picture.

The right tool for the job

As an organisation, we were particularly keen to prevent situations like these, rather than correcting them. I explored how we trained people. I did deep dives with different departments and I investigated our quality assurance functions and how we enacted them. I used rich pictures from Soft Systems Methodology to explore multiple perspectives. The pictures captured the reality of situations in a cartoon-like way. They showed things like relationships, influences, elements of the situation and, importantly, the thoughts and feelings of those involved. They displayed the information in a non-threatening way and allowed things to emerge that we might never have articulated verbally. They first appeared childish to me but over time, the more I used them, the more powerful I found them for exposing elements such as power, influence and the social and political dimensions in a situation.

I used causal loop diagrams from System Dynamics to explore problematic situations. They enabled me to graphically represent the interrelationships in a way that brought new insights to light. I realised that displaying information differently opened up a whole new understanding of how things were connected and how they influenced one another. I also routinely used the VSM to explore where complexity was not being managed well and as a result there was some low-level chaos reoccurring daily. The VSM helped me to understand why this was happening. I was able to contemplate actions for improvement.

I also used Critical Systems Heuristics to explore sources of motivation in our situations. This was another approach that looked quite simplistic to me when I first came across it. Yet I soon changed my mind after using it. The approach consists of a framework for reflective practice, centred around boundary critique. It encouraged me to explore the judgements that were being made. Looking at sources of motivation, control, knowledge and legitimacy gave me a set of questions and permission to explicitly challenge the current situation and contemplate an 'ought to be' state.

Rich pictures never really went down very well with others, at first. People thought they were childish in appearance, just as I had originally thought. When engaging very serious senior scientists they were not always the right tool for me to use in this particular organisation. However, later in my journey, in my systems change work, they became the star of the show. Causal loop diagrams, however, were again, as they were in commissioning, a big hit. People could see their worth very quickly. The VSM was also very useful to me but was not the approach to easily explain to others. I used it mainly for my insights and to guide my discussions around improvements and change activities.

Commissioning again

I really loved working for that NHS organisation, but I had a deep sense that I wanted to do more and on a wider scale. I wanted to help more people and support the NHS to be even better at what it did. I felt that only supporting one small area of the NHS was maybe not the best I could do. I needed to spread my wings wider to share stories about systems thinking, which I hoped might infect others to get curious about the discipline. I moved on but kept all of the amazing friends I made there.

I moved back into commissioning and at the same time I was contemplating whether self-employment as a business consultant might be for me. My portfolio of work was huge and interesting. I covered urgent care, ageing well and a few other things too. I jumped straight in, applying systems thinking to the areas of pathway redesign, bringing care for older people closer to their homes, improving care homes, developing minor ailments schemes, exploring how intravenous antibiotics might be given in a community setting, and looking at what could be done to support Accident and Emergency departments by improving the range of services available to people as they turned up. I looked at the effectiveness of ambulatory medical assessment clinics and whether we might introduce urgent care practitioners to the area.

I managed GP out-of-hours contracts and developed strategies for improvements. I explored GP practice 'did not attend' rates and undertook a review of community nursing. I also looked at the reasons for older people falling and how we could support them better. I had responsibility for allocating over 75s funding and how we could support the frail elderly and I explored whether community geriatricians could be a valuable asset for the area. This is not a full list, so you might imagine that I had plenty of opportunities to put my systems thinking into practice and I had the autonomy I needed to move all streams of work forward in a way that I thought was best. It was stimulating and interesting and I again appreciated the autonomy I had and the trustful relationships I worked in and around. Without them, the work would never have moved forward. As you might imagine, the work was all cross-organisational and the span of groups and organisations and networks involved was wide and varied. Many were across different regions and so I was, once again, working concurrently at multiple scales in the system.

Coordinating across boundaries

Like much work of this cross-organisational and cross-boundary nature, I saw that there were challenges in establishing common governance mechanisms or ones that were aligned to enable the work to progress. Clear boundaries of responsibility were not always initially fully agreed and yet we all pulled together to get things done. One of the most disruptive system 'sicknesses' I encountered in the work during this time, which I recognised with my more technical systems thinking lens, was about coordination, or System 2 in the VSM.

We can get oscillations in the performance of our operations, and we need a way to dampen them down. These are things we put in place to stop different operations from causing chaos for one another. It might be something like a timetable or schedule (which was obviously missing in the case of the vans in the last organisation). It might be an IT system that helps us communicate our actions, decisions or requests. It can be anything that seeks to bring some harmony into how the operations work. With all of the interconnected and interdependent operational elements of health and care, you can imagine that this area can be a bit of a minefield.

I saw information that never passed from one place to another. Computer systems that did not talk to each other, so feedback loops were not closed between one part of the system and another. I saw IT systems that hindered, rather than supported the work of nurses and social workers. I saw conflicting guidance and protocols. I saw scheduling that was not supportive to the people it needed to serve. I saw people solving the same simple issues over and over again. I saw interface issues between services. I saw disruption between teams. The list was endless.

One example I came across repeatedly was when older people had a plethora of health and care services visiting them in their own homes, sometimes in an erratic, uncoordinated and intrusive way. I even stood one day with a senior nurse as she shooed everyone out of an older person's home, to give her a rest and some breathing space. She removed five people from the woman's home that day. Who on earth thought it was ok for five different people from different services to descend upon an older woman, who had just come out of the hospital and was trying to get orientated back in her own home, at the same time? Probably no one as it was no one's job to co-ordinate everyone's visits. They were all done separately, by different people, often in different organisations. At what point did any of the people turn around and think this is not ok . On that day, I can tell you that they did not. They just kept coming and we snapped.

The water we swim in

One thing I am very sure about is that mechanisms for coordination become almost invisible in an organisation. It is the water we swim around in every day that we do not realise gives our work situations life or makes them sick. People tend to assume coordination happens automatically and needs no attention. As a result, it is completely overlooked. There is often little attention or consideration about how it is working.

Without good coordination, our working world can quickly become chaotic. It can cause erratic workloads, staff feeling like they are bobbing around alone in a small boat in the middle of a crashing ocean, inter-team disputes and recurring low-level issues. What I see most is that it causes people to reinvent the wheel over and over again, day in, day out. I know with some certainty if coordination is seen as important and proper attention is given to it, improvements can be easily made, often with no financial outlay.

Coordination is a hugely powerful place of intervention to make improvements happen. It sits right in front of people's eyes, often growling in their faces and yet, at the same time, is completely invisible. It is as if it does not count. What I see very often is that people dismiss suggestions of change and improvement that are about coordination. They prefer instead to opt for something deemed to be grander and/or more innovative, for example, a complete redesign or restructure. My experiences are that these are often unnecessary but because there has been a problem for so long, there is an assumption that some kind of big-bang change is required to improve. I often think that senior managers can default to this option intentionally at times. To improve a situation by easier means could feel embarrassing for them, because if it were that easy, it would have been done already, right?

Systems thinking for evaluation

You rarely work alone in the NHS, and with my background in pharmacy, it was inevitable that I would end up doing projects with pharmacists at some point. I teamed up with a pharmacist colleague to evaluate a minor ailments scheme. It was known that it was quite under-utilised. What was not known was whether it could improve or whether it just needed decommissioning. It was an interesting area of work and Richard and I set off together to see what we could find out.

We looked at all the usual things you might consider when evaluating a scheme like this. We did a needs assessment. We considered the demographics, the postal districts of those registered with the scheme, what days people attended, the uptake profile throughout the lifecycle of the scheme, the level of pharmacy provider engagement, the number of pharmacy consultations and the age range of the patients, action taken by the pharmacists and levy status for items supplied. We looked at presenting conditions, types of medication supplied, monthly variation and costs. We explored year-on-year trends and patient feedback. It was a comprehensive piece of work. We also considered the viability of the scheme.

We used the VSM as our guide and we looked at the sub-systems included in the model.

System 1 - the primary operations
We looked at what the scheme actually did, and what the local area needed it to do and considered whether the scheme was delivering value to its external environment.

System 2 - coordination
We looked for weaknesses in coordination. Did people understand what the scheme was, how it worked and did the scheme have things in place to make it run smoothly?

System 3 - Day to day delivery
We explored whether the scheme had adequate resources and whether it was being appropriately performance managed.

System 3* - monitoring
We looked at what monitoring was being done and whether outcomes of the monitoring were being fed back into the operational management of the scheme.

System 4 – intelligence about the environment and the future development of the scheme
We considered if there was an appropriate balance between managing the daily operations of the scheme and considering its future development. What might it have to deal with in the coming months?

System 5 – how the scheme was governed
We scrutinised the governance of the scheme and explored what purpose and identity the scheme had, both through our eyes and the eyes of the patients. Of course, you will not be surprised to hear that both of those perspectives were different.

We explored the emergent properties of the service and we looked at how things worked over time, rather than a single snapshot. Together, Richard and I took the time to contrast dynamic complexity (the relationships between things) with detail complexity (details about things).

It was not the second-order reflexive kind of evaluation I might do today, where I consider my role in the evaluation to a greater degree, but it fitted with my thinking at the time and gave us the information we required.

One of the first things we found was that the commissioning organisation believed the scheme's purpose was to encourage people to consult pharmacy staff as a first point of call for a minor ailment. GP practices, pharmacy staff and patients, however, perceived that the scheme was predominantly only for patients who would not normally pay prescription charges. We knew at that point we had some work to do on the identity of the scheme. We also found that the time the scheme was used was predominantly in-hours, i.e., 9-5 Monday to Friday. This was contrary to perceptions that existed before the scheme started. It had been previously thought that the purpose of the scheme might be to give an alternative to the current out-of-hours services, which again indicated differences in the perceived purpose of the scheme.

We also found that the scheme was under-publicised. Plus, the data capture process for pharmacists, which was done on paper, did not exactly mirror the data capture process on the IT system, so we knew we had some small areas of coordination failure that could be improved.

We then went on to explore whether there were oscillations in the performance of the scheme. None were found. The uptake and engagement of pharmacies was on a slow upward trend. The only oscillations were due to seasonal variations in demand, such as the increased demand for hay fever products, during summer. The lack of oscillations indicated that the scheme, whilst not realising its full potential at present, was in control and it was providing value. We did, however, recognise a degree of low-level chaos with feedback from patients to GP practices. Some patients were confused about the scheme and in turn, made the GP receptionists confused. It was a vicious cycle of incorrect information that was impacting the scheme's potential effectiveness. This was an easy feedback loop to correct, so we were confident we could make an improvement.

The scheme was well resourced and quality monitoring was routinely undertaken. Quality of leadership was good, although there was potential for further pharmacies to be recruited into the scheme. We also concluded that the scheme had strong governance. Overall, we found that the scheme had a bit of an identity issue, and it could benefit from more pharmacies being recruited. People who used the scheme liked it but not many people knew about it. There was some confusion about the initiative that caused variation in take-up over different geographical areas. It was feasible to expect that if the scheme were to be commissioned for a longer period it would continue to be useful. If the expectation, however, were to improve the performance of the scheme significantly, then it might not meet those expectations.

What was most important was that I had something to guide my exploration and a set of systems thinking ideas to query various elements of the scheme. It brought a different dimension to the work and was recognised as strengthening our evaluation. I thoroughly enjoyed working on this with Richard and that inner peace should be recognised. We had a structured way forward in an otherwise complex situation and we used it well.

'So, why do people not know about these things, Pauline?' Someone in my organisation asked me. Well, systems thinking can sound like a very technical thing to some people. For example, much of the writing about the VSM was done back in the 1960s and 1970s. Few people are writing about it even today in terms that can be more easily understood in our current contexts. Those who do know how to use it, know that they possess a powerful skillset and many do not want to pass that on, as it might mean they lose their competitive advantage, particularly if they run their own consultancy business. For that reason, there are far too few texts that explain these ideas in easy-to-understand ways with examples. The other reason is that when you apply the VSM and other systems thinking ideas, it can reveal very deep insights about the situation you are engaging with. Some of those insights might not be positive. People generally do not want to air their dirty washing in public and so it can be difficult to talk in any detail about work you have done. For that reason, it is difficult to openly share case studies and experiences fully.

Relaying this message to others in the organisation brought me to a place where I felt that I wanted to spread the word about the usefulness of engaging in systems thinking and the additional rigour it can bring to your work. I knew I could not talk about my case studies in any great detail, for the reasons of confidentiality that I have just mentioned. I also knew that I did not want to focus on the heavy academics of systems thinking. There are plenty of resources that do that already. I wondered if there was another way to support people to get similar powerful insights without having to go through long academic courses, as I had done. Not everyone has the time, money or desire to do that.

Was it possible? Surely, there had to be a way to support people to engage in systems thinking that was less taxing. After all, it had not taken long for the basics of the VSM to stop being a grumbling, growling monster, standing alone in the darkened corner of my systems thinking party. It had become my vibrant dancing partner and I was now dancing with it right in the middle of the floor, and sometimes, it really is murder on the dancefloor, so you need a good partner.

This was something I was soon to explore. But first, I needed to probe deeper into elements of systems thinking that had been puzzling me.

Chapter 4: A new start line

Down the rabbit hole

I had been down the rabbit hole for eighteen months. It was cold, dark and muddy. Bits of grass were poking into my squinting, blurry eyes and I kept tripping over gnarly, knotted roots of various shrubs and trees. Umph! Down I went again, grazing my hands. Blimey, why on earth did I come down here? My knees were scraped and bloody and my feet were swollen and throbbing. My arms were raw where I had brushed against the sides of this murky, hot burrow. It was the VSM that made me do it. It made me jump down this hole, headfirst. There was no time for preparation. I had given no consideration to what it might feel like. Nothing. Down I went, naively unaware.

I was contemplating the concept of timely information exchanges for making viable systems effective. Someone in the world of systems thinking had said to me that if the information got to the right place at the right time, the VSM should work effectively. I did not believe this and thought the statement was incorrect. Why? Because nearly every piece of work that I had done, people said things like: we didn't know, we weren't told, we don't have the information or we can't get the information. Nearly every time, I located the information very easily and it was at the tip of their fingers. Right there, right in front of them. I was baffled. The information was visible, yet invisible, both at the same time, like a bizarre optical illusion playing havoc with their eyes. That was what made me do it. Along with academic shrieks that information does not flow and my desire to pass on insights about the usefulness of systems thinking to others. That is what started my slow and perilous journey down this pitch-black rabbit hole on the next stage of my journey.

I was reviewing the work on hospital discharge that I had done between 2008 and 2012 again. The work was a long time before I went down this current rabbit hole, but I often looked back on past pieces of work and scrutinised them further as I developed my systems practice. What had really been happening in the work at the time? What had I, and others, actually done when things worked well? What had we done when things had not worked so well? Were the things that I thought had been happening, really happening? Had the bits that worked well, worked well for the reasons I believed? Or because of something else?

Some parts of the work had gone really well indeed, I reflected. Others, not so well and I wanted to know more about why. I queried whether I had been projecting the VSM onto the situation at the time and I wanted to challenge myself again to see what I thought now that time had passed. I went back through the programme of work in painstaking detail and said to myself, 'What happened here? What did people actually do to make this work?' and, 'What did I think at the time was happening here?' and 'Where is my evidence for that?'

As we all know, there is a difference between reflecting-in-action and reflecting-on-action, when the memory can play tricks on us and we open up the potential to see what we want to see, rather than what actually happened. I had, however, made comprehensive notes of my reflections at the time and now I was looking for discrepancies. I was looking for any evidence of projection and bias and for areas of unknowns that I did not notice at the time. I was deeply scrutinising my past work and leaving no stone unturned.

I had studied the VSM on an Open University undergraduate module, a few years before that piece of work. I was not as deep into the academics of the model back then, so I was interested to see if my perspective had changed.

Communication breakdown

I deeply contemplated the words communication and information whilst down the rabbit hole. What did they really mean? What did they mean to different groups of people? What did they mean to me? Most importantly, I contemplated why, even when information exchanges were fast, they might still not be effective. There are many things to consider, of course. Do people know that there is a message to pick up? How do they hear the message? What raises the alarm? Are people speaking the same language when they communicate? How do they interact with each other? Is the interaction effective? Is the key message drowned out by other information? Does the information need filtering out so that people can concentrate on what is most important? Does it need amplifying? How is the information interpreted? Do we check how it is interpreted? Do we check it is interpreted as intended and acted on as intended? That is how it started, the precarious jaunt down the rabbit hole to explore what communication and information meant.

I looked specifically at the aspect of hospital discharge that included repatriations of a patient from one area of the country to another. Back then, this could cause significant delays for the patient. The hospital in which they resided would be eager for them to be discharged. The area they were going to would be even more eager not to bring them back too quickly and put excess pressure on already limited care home places and stretched home support teams.

At the time, I remembered walking quite slowly down a wide, shiny white corridor of a hospital I had never visited before, taking in the clinical and rather empty atmosphere. I was always nervous about going to new places, but I forced myself to do it. I dealt with the anxiety of driving to a new town, navigating the confusing hospital car parks, grappling to find the right change to give me long enough on the parking meter, and figuring out which building I should be in after walking around in circles for at least 15 minutes. That in itself was exhausting, and I had ended up wandering around like a lost sheep down this huge white corridor.

It was a fluke that I had found it, the door to the office for the hospital discharge team. They had known I was coming, though, so there might have been a nice cup of tea when I got there. I tried the door. It was locked so I tapped gently, not wanting to startle anyone. Silence. I tried the door again. Nothing. I tapped again. Nothing. I got out my phone and called the number of the head of the team and I heard a light ringing behind the door. So, their phone was in there, but where were they?

Caught up in a discharge meeting more than likely, or desperately trying to grab a break in the middle of their punishing shift. Then I heard a shuffle inside the door and what I thought was a sniffle. I leaned closer into the door and heard it again. 'Hello', I said very gently. 'It's Pauline Roberts. Are you ok?' The door clicked open, and I stepped inside, making sure I closed and locked the door again behind me.

There were tears and apologies. An exhausted person sat in front of me, slumped at their desk. They had done a long, draining shift the day before because they were short of staff. They had taken on extra duties and worked long hours. After crawling home at the end of it, they had been called at home, late at night, by a manager because one thing had not been done. They were back in the hospital, working at 8am the next day. The person I was standing next to was exhausted, demotivated, demoralised and broken. She cried and cried. I put the kettle on and asked her to tell me about it. We talked and talked. I helped her look through her schedule for the day and rearrange things so that we could have a couple of hours together and we went to lunch. After lunch, I asked how I could help to make the repatriation situation easier at her end. That had been the start of a beautiful reciprocal arrangement between two different geographical areas that needed to work together.

Repatriating patients from one area to another requires all involved to work together to put arrangements in place in a way that considers the patient as central and also considers pressures on services, care homes and home support. I had always encountered this as a problematic area, with little reciprocation and a lot of game playing. I was told that the game playing as it was so labelled, had been going on for at least ten years before that point, probably longer. But what was wrong? Was it that each side did not have enough information to make the arrangements required? I did not doubt that this happened, but in the instances I explored this had not been the case. The information was readily available. It was understood, not drowned out by other things and had been there, right in front of people. I must be something of an explorer as my instinct was to keep digging.

I found burnt-out care staff, frazzled nurses on wards and distraught managers with the weight of the world on their shoulders. We talked, observed and shared stories.

We discussed our challenges. Then, after a period of offloading about what was not working, we explored opportunities together. The hospital discharge teams in each area were put in direct contact with each other and we investigated the opportunities for us all, together.

To cut a very much longer story short, what we came up with was a reciprocal arrangement and a closer relationship between the discharge teams. An agreement that did not favour one hospital over another but considered both as equal partners in an almost impossible situation. A reciprocal arrangement that held each side to timescales and actions agreed upon by all. It was not perfect for anyone but it was fair. Well, as fair as it could be in a troubled, unjust arena of health and care, that had been stripped of cash and run into the ground for years. Each team got to work on its own hierarchy to get its own chief executive's agreement to the inclusion of the agreement in a Joint Protocol for the Transfer of Care.

It was not easy, but it worked. It took away a lot of arguing. The chief executives from two neighbouring areas signed up and remained signed up over the next three years. The result? Well, this had been part of a whole programme of activity that I undertook so we cannot attribute any successes directly to this, but it did contribute to a delayed discharge figure lower than the regional and national average for the three years. Not bad for a large teaching hospital. It also attracted the attention of the Strategic Health Authority which had been closely watching our hospital discharge work and wanted to understand how we did it. I do not know what happened after that as primary care trusts, the type of organisation I worked for, were eventually disbanded, and I moved on. However, my Aha! moment in all of this came when I was down that dark and murky rabbit hole.

Was the success of our work about information? No, not really. It was more to do with reciprocation, the relationships between the teams and the way we made meaning of the situation and the ask from both sides together. We explored it together. We exposed the issues and what it meant for each party, together. We knew what the trade-offs were, and we talked to each other openly and honestly about them. By forming a personal bond with other teams outside of the boundaries of our local health system, we enabled the relationships. We created a channel of meaningful interaction. There had been personal investments on both sides - people could clearly see the benefits of reciprocating and collaborating. You could say that this is an information exchange. That might be true, but for me, the power of the relationship was when we made meaning of the situation together. We explored each other's perspectives and understood the gains and downfalls for all of us. It made me reflect on the power of enabling interaction and deliberate reciprocation strategies. I deeply embedded these in my systems practice as I reflected on what had happened.

These were not the only things that came out of this work, but they were pertinent because I originally believed that it was purely a lack of information that caused some of the problems. I started by contemplating how we could make the information exchange faster. I did not necessarily find the answers I originally sought down the rabbit hole, but I did find something else. Enlightening little gems, sparkling fearlessly in the darkness.

My reaction to this was quite weird. You might think that I would be elated at my discoveries but that was not my initial reaction. My newfound insights, at first, felt devastating. Yes, you read that right. They felt devastating. My heart sank like a heavy stone in a crystal clear yet very deep pond. I thought I had got it so completely wrong. I had a real moment of trembling fear that everything I had done up to this point had been built on incorrect thinking about information exchanges. What did that mean for the work? For the people involved? Would it be my fault if everything else failed or started to go wrong? I was mortified. I remember at the time talking to a friend about it online. I was distressed, and upset, and felt lost and disorientated. I thought that all of my work had been proven wrong and that I could never move forward. I had an uncomfortable throbbing in my head, a tingling in my fingers and my heart intensely pounded as my body flooded with adrenaline. I came to tears on more than one occasion and wondered if I could ever make a go of this systems thinking thing, despite being so far along in my systems thinking journey already. Never before had I questioned my own abilities, mindset and work as I did at the time of coming out of the rabbit hole. It took several weeks before I would even contemplate systems thinking again.

This part of my journey was emotion-fuelled and turbulent. At the same time, it was exciting and motivating. What a jumble of feelings to come to terms with. I guess a lot of systems thinking practitioners go through this on their journey. That crippling fear that at some stage you have been completely wrong, even though that assumption is completely irrational. What it did bring to light, however, was that others might experience this too and it became one of the inspirations for the framing of this book as the sharing of a journey.

Once I composed myself, I continued consolidating my academic learning in systems thinking with my experiences in the workplace and indeed in my life. I was firmly established in my own style of practising at this point. I had come a long way already, although it felt like a brand-new start line.

The other side of the rabbit hole

That is how I felt as I arrived at the exit of the rabbit hole. I tentatively poked the top of my head out into the blinding, warm sunshine and decided that despite the pain, I had arrived at some relevant insights. I already had an established systems thinking approach of my own at this point and I decided it was time for an update and re-branding in my own mind. I thought of my approach as partly being about Creating the Conditions for Change, which I will talk more about in the next chapter. But first, a little more about how my journey felt at that point in time.

Alone in the workplace

It was now 2015 and I was routinely sharing my insights on social media as I worked out loud, iteration after iteration. I talked about how I had experimented with my systems practice by blending the VSM with other systems thinking approaches. I originally called this approach my blended systems thinking approach to change and improvement. I brought together tools, techniques and concepts from several different approaches. I tried them out, learned a lot, and then tried them out again. I had both successes and failures. I enjoyed sharing my stories. As my determination to make improvements grew ever stronger and my use of some little-known approaches developed, however, I felt like an outcast in the workplace.

Although I held a high enough management position to have great autonomy, I felt like I stood alone, misunderstood and under-utilised. I used a different work language from everyone else. My thinking did not fit with most of the people around me and work became a very lonely place. I felt like I no longer fit. People around me did show some interest in systems thinking and in developing their own systems practice, but they did not want to become as deeply embedded in it as I was. It was not the trendy-sounding approach that people might think of today. It was still relatively unheard of and rarely talked about. People had far too many work demands to stop and consider a different way of thinking about things. I had no one to talk to about the insights I was gaining, and I felt like I wandered for some time in the world of an immeasurably deep abyss. I felt that my options for fitting in could become increasingly limited and I wondered if I would ever feel comfortable at work again.

Nevertheless, I continued to develop my systems practice, emphasising a specific focus on empathetic leadership. But again, I felt that I had nowhere to go with it. Eventually, and I have to say quite erratically, I stepped into the world of being self-employed and started my own limited company. Oh boy, it was a turbulent start and not a recommendation for the direction of your journey that I would give lightly. I only wish I had been better prepared.

Going it alone

'I absolutely cannot do this!' I thought to myself. I had just read what I needed to do to set up a limited company. 'No way. I just can't!' But I took a deep breath, took it step by step and I did it anyway. I set up my own limited company as a systems thinking practitioner. It took me a while. I was a sole trader for some time first, until I got my head around everything I needed to do, such as setting up appropriate insurance and getting an accountant. This was completely unchartered waters for me and something I had never even contemplated before. In fact, even when setting the company up I would often think to myself, 'What on earth are you doing?'

'It won't work, Pauline. People don't want that kind of consultancy. No one even knows what systems thinking is, never mind wanting to hire a consultant to help them with it. You're mad! You've got a great job with good pay and good holidays. You're moving up the hierarchy. What on earth are you doing?' My friends really did not understand what I was doing. Truth be told, neither did I, but I did not tell them that. They were right, I did have a good secure job, good money, good holidays and plenty of perks. It was comfortable and I found life quite easy. But I had an overwhelming desire to continue on my journey, even if I did not really know where that desire was coming from or where I would end up.

'Just enjoy work! Take advantage of the rest if you're bored' people would keep telling me. I cannot tell you how annoying that was. When times were quiet and I was bored, it was not a rest for me. It made me anxious and irritable. It made me lose my sense of meaning and purpose. It was not aligned with the identity I wanted for myself, and it made me feel physically sick. I could not get people to understand this. I knew that being self-employed would be hard. It was highly probable that I would fail. I would have no supporters, of that I was sure, and I was taking a big risk financially. I did not have a partner or family around me to support me if things did not work out. I was not rich. I did not have a large raft of money to float along on. But, for some reason, which is still partly unknown to me, I still wanted to go ahead. I wanted to continue with my perilous journey across the bridge, despite the odds against me.

Pauline Roberts

In the deep end

I did it. I dived in, headfirst. Straight into the deep end of the dark blue pool from the highest board. I did not build my business slowly, alongside a job, which would have been the more sensible option. I just impulsively dived straight in, following my gut instinct. I was lucky, I think. My first client was great and ended up being a long-term NHS client. I was with them on and off, for around four years, alongside other clients. They took to me like I took to them. They helped me get established and supported me as much as I supported them. They even looked after me as one of their own when my sister died, sending flowers and cards.

I helped my clients to understand how to engage with different perspectives and why there were differences of opinion about what was happening in their situations. I worked with them to understand the implications of their judgements. I helped them to understand structures and the idea of feedback in systems. I pointed out where patterns of system behaviour were at play. I helped them to identify variety imbalances that were creating havoc in their services. Together, we used a multiple criteria analysis to help decide what changes might be systemically desirable and culturally feasible for them, which was another idea I brought with me from the Open University. I introduced the idea of engaging with small-scale prototyping and experimentation, rather than jumping into larger-scale pilot projects. My clients have not always gone with my suggestions. There were times when I was quite definitely rejected and ridiculed, but more often than not, most clients were willing to give things a try or at the very least, they were curious.

I worked with clients to consider how they might design services from scratch, based on the needs and purposes driving demand. We worked together to re-frame situations and consider organisational identity. We built capacity by focusing on interconnections and interactions and built capabilities by learning together. Sometimes, the work went further than the transformation of services and departments.

'That was cathartic', said as she slumped back into a chair. 'I thought it was all me. My fault. I was just getting it wrong and couldn't cope.' This was a common reaction when I worked with people. So many people take the responsibility for the failure of a large complex situation on their shoulders. They lose sight of the fact that decision upon decision had been made before they even came along. Structure after structure had been changed. Funding had been reduced, staff had been left to cope without enough resources and no one really knew what direction they were going in anymore.

'How on earth could it be all you, Jackie? All of this? How could it possibly be all your fault? Do you think this happened in the last twelve months? This has been created over many years. It is not for you to take the blame for it. All you need to do is find the bits you can do something about, so let's go!' So many clients blame themselves. It is such wasted energy.

'Ok, well, where do we start? I'm so overwhelmed. I have no idea where to start looking to make a change.' Jackie put her head in her hands. I put the kettle on. This was feeling familiar!

Supporting my clients to observe

A key benefit that came from my style of systems practice was around helping my clients to observe. Not just see, but truly observe and understand what they might be looking at. We are all susceptible to system blindness, where we stop seeing what is right in front of our noses. It is important to work out how we might make those things visible to us again. I often found that it helped my clients when I prompted them to look at specific things. Certainly, this had the potential to guide them in a particular direction, but some direction is better than no direction when you are learning to observe. I found that my observations came very much from instinct and by sensing what was going on around me. I could feel the energy around me very easily and that helped guide me in the right direction. This is not something I could easily and convincingly encourage my clients to do though, so common things to focus on to try out their observation skills was a good place to start.

If I knew the client well and we had a good trusting relationship, I would start them off by observing things about themselves. If I knew them less well, however, and had not yet had time to build up that kind of relationship, I would help them to focus on things they could observe in the workplace. Let's take a closer look at the things we considered using the work with Jackie as an example.

Boundaries and context

Many of my clients did not realise that they often unconsciously imposed conceptual boundaries around situations. We can do this intentionally to enable us to focus on a scenario while remaining aware that we have deliberately excluded some elements. It is when we are not aware that it can become problematic.

Jackie's team had been quite inwardly focused. They had put an imaginary boundary around their own organisation and tended not to think much beyond that. Jackie and I looked at what was happening in the wider environment, outside her organisation. There was a large-scale transformation going on across the whole of health and care in the city. Incredibly, people in her teams knew very little about it. They knew something was happening. They did not know what and it was unnerving them. They had consciously decided not to engage with it because it felt too overwhelming. The feeling they described to me was as if they were walking tentatively across quicksand, believing that the minute they acknowledged they were walking across it, their feet would start sinking, followed by the rest of their body, with no one to pull them out.

I was not concerned that a conceptual boundary had been drawn. That was quite natural and normal. What worried me was that the service and teams were not considering the impact of the environmental changes on their internal world and preparing for what might come next. There was a distinct lack of strategic planning because they were overwhelmed and paralysed with fear. Their paralysis prevented them from even contemplating changing their own practices and I knew this was a sure way to get into deep trouble, very quickly.

Identity and purpose

Something very important to Jackie's teams was that they maintained their professional identity throughout any changes. This was something Jackie had not fully contemplated before. She assumed people would just go with the flow of whatever change was happening. On talking to her teams, who were social workers, they were deeply worried. I could see it in their faces. They were concerned that their professional identity would be impacted by the more generalist roles that they had heard discussed on the grapevine. It was a time of great uncertainty and there was a desperate need to create the right conditions to nurture the teams as they moved forwards.

The overarching purpose of their team might well change. That would potentially change its identity. In turn, that would potentially change their identity and they had not chosen that change. Imagine that – you studied and worked your whole life to be a particular type of professional. Suddenly, some transformation, that you know little about and have certainly not influenced, might change your everyday purpose and as a result, your identity. And all of this was not your choice. I do not know about you, but I would be pretty worried about that. They were. I could see it. Their rationale for being unnerved was sound.

Framing and motivation

The teams framed the situation that was upon them as something that was being imposed. 'It's like a giant monster, Pauline. It's coming to gobble us up. We know it.' They were trying their very best to avoid it, hide from it even, but it was coming, no matter what. Their framing of it as a monster drove their fears. Their fears drove their framing and they were caught in a feedback loop, a vicious cycle spiralling their concerns out of control. Pinpointing how people frame things can tell you a lot about how they feel about a situation and is key to observe, as it can reveal so much.

If only Jackie and her teams had known before I came along that reframing the situation as something more positive could help them immensely. Re-framing a situation can open up your perspective and help you see a situation with a completely new lens. Just changing the question from: 'How is this going to make things worse for me?' to 'What opportunities will this give me?' can be immensely powerful, although I do admit that persuading people to consider re-framing is quite a skill. Get it wrong and it can undermine and patronise as it appears to trivialise people's experiences. But, working with people to enable the reframing to occur more naturally can be a useful skill for a practitioner. It certainly opened up a world of potential for my client.

Unwritten rules of the game

The unwritten rules of the game in Jackie's teams were to keep busy, keep out of the way and hope that the monster did not catch you. Do not upset any senior managers, or you would be out. There are always unwritten rules at play in any work environment. They are the things that people know about, but no one dare say for fear of being classed as negative or paranoid. Identifying unwritten rules can be a very revealing skill for a practitioner. It helps you to get to the heart of issues quickly, cutting through the noise of words and revealing powerful patterns. In fact, it is so powerful that I dedicate a whole workshop to it nowadays and have developed resources for my clients to prompt them about common patterns to look out for.

Rules of the game can be formal or informal, although more often than not they are informal. They can be overt or covert, although they are often covert. How are those who are surviving well in the situation manoeuvring the change and in particular, the politics? I thought back again to my days in the primary care trust when my friend said she would teach me, 'how to deal with this bloody lot'. She knew the unwritten rules of the game and played them well.

'What are the unwritten rules of the game here, Jackie?' I asked.

I swear she nearly fell off her seat. Her mouth dropped as if I had just mouthed a string of obscenities into her ear.

'Who is surviving this well?' No answer.

'What are they doing that these teams aren't?'

I never did get a real answer, although I think she had it right there, in the very front of her mind.

Spotting fear

Of course, among all the change was the perception of why it was happening.

'They want rid of us. They hate us. They'll get rid of me the minute they can. They have wanted rid of me for ages.'

I heard these things repeatedly. Fear was clearly at play and Stafford Beer's VSM came to mind, yet again. If, when using the model, we seek to reduce things like unwanted demand, then when it came to people, I felt quite sure we needed to reduce unhelpful levels of fear. Dampen it down to a manageable level.

People's perceptions play havoc when they are scared. They project their own meaning onto things, and it can easily get out of hand. I have known many people leave their jobs unnecessarily because of this. Heck, I have even done it myself in the past. We get caught up in our thoughts. Our mindset gets stuck. Our reactions are lightning-quick and razor sharp and before we know it, we have made a decision based on our fears. When undertaking change, we do not just need to make structural changes. We need to understand what the change means for the people involved and involve them in making meaning of it at the earliest possible stages to prevent things like fear from getting out of control. This is often given lip service but not very often enacted in any meaningful way, in my experience. Spotting different kinds of fear and when your teams are suffering are very important patterns to observe.

Values and ethics

I suspected that values and ethics might come into play in the answer about the unwritten rules of the game that was never given by Jackie. Those with strong values and ethics can often come off badly during change. This can often be because people stick rigidly to their values and ethics and do not flex at all. That is perfectly fine, as long as there is not a simple compromise that could have maintained people's usual level of ethics and values and it was missed because they were blinded by their perceptions and fears. It can be useful to explore whether this is playing out during any changes you are making. Finding a simple compromise can be all it takes to smooth things over. Do you talk to your teams about their ethics and values when you are making change?

Where my clients are, in terms of their ethics and values, is of their choosing. I can point things out to them, but it is up to them if they do anything about it. I find that is the best way to leave it. I am there to advise, not to take responsibility for their actions or inaction and I cannot go to battle in every poor situation I come across.

People first, then organisation

Back in my days in pharmaceuticals, I was given the book, *Fitting the Task to the Human* by Kroemer and Grandjean as part of an extensive programme of human error reduction training I was undertaking. It flipped my thinking to people first, organisation second and it has been that way ever since, albeit in slightly different ways and different contexts. I wonder how much the financial cuts prevented the teams from putting humans first, including themselves. Spotting when you are serving the organisation and not the people, is another revealing pattern to look out for.

Influence

'Who or what influences the way you and your teams work, Jackie?' It was easy for her to identify the organisational strategic influences but there is often so much more at play in situations, especially where there is a lot of change happening. Influences might come from places such as management, quality, objectives, budgets, performance targets, hierarchy, and legislation. They can also come from other areas, such as organisational culture, personalities and motivations of individuals. This is where some of the unwritten rules come into play. What influence are they having on your situation? There were some at play in Jackie's situation, but she was keeping them close to her chest.

Seeing the world differently

By this stage, I was routinely trying to help my clients see their world differently, picking up on things that they may have become accustomed to overlooking. When translating the VSM into an approach that was about empathetic, conscious leadership and/ or system leadership, I had now developed a specific focus on what Stafford Beer called the System 3* monitoring sub-system of the model. What I was advocating for was monitoring for effective system characteristics and signs of humanity in our workplaces. For system health.

'Jackie, how do you reward people for collaborating with other teams and organisations?'

As you might imagine, the answer was that they did not. I wondered when and how we had lost sight of these things or whether people ever had sight of them in the first place.

I believed that we needed to disrupt people's own hardwiring about what was important to monitor to enable a different purpose in the work. The purpose of meaningful and fulfilling work, rather than just a task-related, insubstantial purpose. If all we kept monitoring and noticing were imposed targets and task completion, then that is all the work would become. Instead, I advocated monitoring and recognising people for collaborating and reciprocating with others, for sharing and learning. For supporting to heal trauma, both individual and collective. I advocated recognising people for using information to nourish, rather than using it to gain personal power and control. Monitoring for whether people, processes and structures were enabling adaptability or hindering it. I advocated creating human-orientated workplaces and having happy and fulfilled staff. Of course, this was not usually what clients wanted and much of it fell on deaf ears. I felt my approach was right, but the timing was not.

I continued. I was monitoring to see if my clients were giving time for reflection and whether people were taking that time. This was something that I rarely saw happening. I tried to encourage my clients to recognise if they were creating the conditions for people to showcase their gifts and thrive. Was there flexibility, curiosity and co-creation in their everyday work? Was there any evidence of shifts in power and were meaningful relationships being created? I believed wholeheartedly that unless we monitor and recognise different things, we might find that we are not changing habits and are falling back into old patterns of thinking and being, rather than moving forward in a systems thinking informed way. That said, the context of the workplace was generally not in this thinking space and what my clients were looking for was not what I generally wanted to give. I found myself probing for insights but at the same time having to sometimes default to basic project management to deliver the expectations of the client. It felt as if I often had two parallel pieces of work going on in my head at the same time.

Iterating with my systems thinking approach

By now, the insights from working with my clients were feeding even more iterations of my systems practice and my own approach.

Not every contract that I won went smoothly and I was learning more and more about how to gauge when clients really wanted things revealed to them and when they did not. I was always taught that the practitioner is a huge part of the picture when engaging with situations. We have to learn to deal with ourselves as much as dealing with the situation and I was embedding this into the Creating the Conditions for Change approach more and more every day.

It became very important to me, as a practitioner, to engage with a situation in a current rationality-informed way. This meant that I had to tailor my own behaviours to consider that mindset and engage with it effectively. How are people making sense of things? What logic are they using? How are they rationalising what is happening? This was an important pattern for me to spot as a practitioner. I listened to a variety of perspectives. I listened to the kind of language people used. What metaphors they defaulted to. What words they used. What was their tone of voice when using these words? These were all clues I needed to pick up on. It is easy to look like you are spying on people in these situations, so developing trustful relationships with people became vitally important in my systems practice. After all, I wanted to help people, not make them feel like I was spying on them.

It was also important for me to understand where I saw signs of stress, both in the people I was engaging with and within myself. Stress can do all kinds of things to our perceptions and so this was another pattern I needed to spot. Consulting is a stressful business. It is very easy to take on board other people's thoughts and emotions and sometimes it was difficult to shake them off at the end of the day.

I had one occasion in particular when I encountered a situation that did not sit well with my values and ethics. It affected me so badly that I took a month off to recover and shake the feelings off once the work was finished. Anyone who thinks consulting is all glamour, money and flexibility has clearly never done it. In fact, I built into my own development plan actions to specifically look at and consider my responses to the ethics and values of others, particularly when they were not aligned with mine. I took time to notice my triggers and emotional reactions to things I did not agree with. I had to learn a whole new set of reflexes to deploy in the event of those negative reactions arising. I can tell you that it was and still is damned hard to do. It took at least a couple of years to feel like I was getting anywhere with it, and I still have to work hard on it today.

The long-term nature of the work

Over time, as I worked on project after project, with client after client, I realised the long-term nature of some of the actions I was proposing. My recommendations were certainly not one-off tasks. My approach was not, go in – problem solve – come out, with a defined result at the end. It was more of an incremental approach that would form habits and see improvements over time. As a consultant, this became difficult as I tried to gain a balance between what my clients wanted and what I believed they needed. This is a classic problem in consultancy, but with my systems thinking approach, it required far more consideration and I was not sure I was truly able to make it work.

As well as the potential long-term nature of systems thinking work, I also became even more convinced that systems thinking was not something that anyone can do for you. It is something that you need to learn for yourself. It needs to become a habit. An everyday thing. A new way of thinking. Something you eventually do without even knowing it. I felt my heart sinking into the empty pit of my stomach again. What did that mean for the direction of my work? Taking my own advice, I knew I had to pivot and re-focus my business. I wanted to focus on supporting others to do for themselves rather than me going in and advising people about what to do. This was a really scary moment for me, and I did not know whether it would work or even where I might find this kind of work. I did not know whether there was a demand for it, or whether my business would fail because of the nature of what I do.

A key strength of my approach was the contextual understanding it enabled, which was equally applicable to a person as it was to an organisation and beyond, being recursive in nature like the VSM. It was a mixture of tried and tested models, methods, concepts and ideas. I brought unconscious patterns and behaviours into consciousness and focused on nurturing, empathy and compassion instead of competition, self-preservation, game playing and greed. I focused on people. I focused on humanity, and my journey was guiding me much more than I felt I was consciously deciding on the journey.

Explicitly exposing my craft

It felt quite unbelievable that I was now undertaking systems thinking consultancy, training and coaching regularly. I felt that developing informative materials that made my approach accessible for others to use on their own seemed like a reasonable way forward. All of my previous iterations and tribulations with my learning from using systems thinking approaches brought me to this new start line, overflowing with insights to share. My thinking was starting to flip from, 'how do I develop my own style and systems thinking approach' to 'how do I share my approach effectively with others who might not have time to engage intensely with academics?' This was soon to become the next stage of my journey, across yet another bridge.

Pauline Roberts

Part 2: Creating the Conditions for Change

Pauline Roberts

Chapter 5: Creating the Conditions for Change

Pivoting towards sharing my experiences and approach to helping others help themselves was a tricky move. I stumbled a few times on the feelings of discomfort. As I widened my scope of clients, I realised that social change lent itself to this kind of work, and that was neither my forte nor my particular area of interest in the past. I did, however, venture into that new unexplored forest and did some powerful work. This was where I was at the start of this book, in our online interactions.

Navigating a new field was a great test for my approach. My Creating the Conditions for Change materials were an invaluable guide. It is only possible to give a brief overview of them here, but you will still get a good feeling for how I practise.

A marmite response

Whenever I mention that my approach is based on my learning from using the VSM, I receive two kinds of reaction. The first kind is largely from people who dislike the VSM because they perceive it to be an idealistic model to aspire to, which, as we know, is not one of the best ways forward when working in complex situations. This appears to be because:

1. They do not understand the different ways in which the ideas from the VSM can be used. They believe the VSM is merely a model to be followed and therefore, nothing more than an attempt to predict how the future should be.

2. They do realise how it can be used but do not want to consider it alongside their preferred approaches. They actively seek to discredit anything associated with the VSM.

The second kind of reaction has been one of enthusiasm, but people try to jump to the application without doing any groundwork on their own thinking first. This can lead to a trivialisation of the approach as they cannot reap the expected rewards. Understanding our current thinking patterns is a key first step.

The two-sided coin

I often say that my approach is a two-sided coin. However, it is more than that, it is two sides of a coin, wrapped up in a silken cloth of self-development and emerging wisdom.

With many of my clients, I use the VSM in quite a traditional way, as that is what their context and expectations require. I look at the various functions, such as primary operations, coordination, day-to-day delivery, planning for the future and how things are governed. I look at feedback and I explore whether there is requisite variety. A reminder that requisite variety is about having enough responses to deal with the complexity that you have to deal with every day. I look at the patterns of system behaviour that tell me whether there is an issue and I use quite a technical mindset in this element of the exploration. This is one side of the coin.

Alongside that is Creating the Conditions for Change. This is the human focused side of the approach, based on enabling change in complex situations. The aim is to bring humanity back into the work by focusing on what we need and want to feel nourished and fulfilled as we go about our daily tasks. Some of what you will read next will be applicable when you are working as a core member of staff in an organisation. Some of it will be applicable when you are an external consultant. Some of it will be applicable when you are working on place-based systems change. Some of it will be applicable when working on public service improvement and transformation. Some of it will be applicable when you are making improvements in private industry. It is for you to decide which elements are applicable and appropriate for you and when. Each situation is different and may require a different nuanced approach. This is the second side of the coin.

However, there is one very serious element of commonality, whatever the context. That is the development of ourselves as empathetic, conscious, confident and wise human beings. This is the silken cloth that wraps around both sides of the coin and binds it all together. We cannot just work on developing our organisations and then put people with the same mindsets into them and expect coherent change. We must create the conditions that allow people to focus on inner development also, rather than just creating the conditions to support the work. This, I feel, is tipping into a whole new focus on human flourishing and I am in the process of continually developing this element of my work. I focus on creating viability in the culture of situations by encouraging the development of both people and relationships. I may even take a complete turn in my journey in future to put one foot even more firmly into this new territory, but that is for a future phase as I cross the next bridge of development that presents itself as I wander down this exciting pathway.

It is very important that as you are reading the upcoming narrative, you do not go away thinking, 'If we do X, that it says in the materials, we will be a great system leader'. Or, 'If we do Y our change project will work brilliantly, or we will enable systems change'. The considerations presented are to help you understand your situation more fully when attempting to create the conditions to support change. They are not a 'do this!' instruction.

Scaling up

I do not advocate for scaling up the approach per se, but for developing systems thinking and practice habits. These habits are equally applicable to a person, a team, a service, a department, an organisation and across organisations. The actions taken just look slightly different for each of these scenarios.

Developing strong skills in basic systems thinking concepts

I am an advocate for gaining confidence in working on your inner development. This is the cloth binding the two sides of the coin together. Without it, the approach can fall apart. Only you can enable yourself to flourish.

I also advocate for becoming competent in applying basic systems thinking concepts and ideas, very, very well. For example, the idea of feedback and variety management. Being able to consider multiple perspectives, understand interconnections and how to re-frame situations. Understanding that you have blind spots and that you are a human being and will have a different perception of a situation to your colleagues and that you will project your thoughts onto a situation are also important. Almost every time I encounter people using systems thinking approaches who complain they are not making progress, they have forgotten to apply and consider basic systems thinking concepts, principles and ideas. Their old habits kick in and they are back where they started. Almost every single time.

The approach

As I have already mentioned, I was at the point where I wanted and needed to give my clients something more than an overload of verbal information to remember. Too much information can be overwhelming and easy to forget, especially when it is about a new approach. Therefore, I developed materials to support my workshops and interactions with my clients. In many cases, I imagined that my clients would not use the written materials for some time after I had left them. One day, perhaps when something sparked an Aha! moment for them, they would have a reference point to go back to, to support them as they re-explored our work together.

I developed an infographic called the Systems Thinking Change Wheel, a 20-page A4 booklet to explain the questions and prompts that the wheel puts forward and a set of 120 action cards to help me facilitate a deep exploration of a situation with my client. The action cards do not tell people what to do, but they give concepts, ideas and prompts about things to consider when you want to create the conditions for change in a situation.

Each element has a story behind it about why I have included it. It was the dark and dirty rabbit hole that I went down that made me develop the supplementary materials. I am still, to this day, not sure whether it was a good or bad idea to create them. On the one hand, they give strong visual aids to help people as they are getting to grips with the ideas. They have them for their own reference afterwards. On the other hand, people can end up trying to bypass the thinking stage of the work and use the materials as a shortcut to an end point. That does not usually yield any kind of meaningful outcome and can often fail in the long run. The shortcut then ends up taking people twice as long and sometimes they never get to where they are going because they picked up and ran with what they thought were tools to get them to a destination quicker. The clue is in the name, systems THINKING. You cannot bypass the thinking element, or you risk ending up right back where you started.

The Systems Thinking Change Wheel

I have refined the systems thinking change wheel over the years, and this is version 5, from 2022.

Describing the infographic

The systems thinking change wheel is an infographic that sets out six areas for consideration when creating the conditions for change. It does not mean 'do these things'. It means, 'explore these things and come to your own judgement about them in the situation you are engaging with'.

The six areas are identified by the different coloured segments in the wheel. Each segment has an inner and outer area. The inner area is the key area of focus. The outer area, further things to consider within that segment.

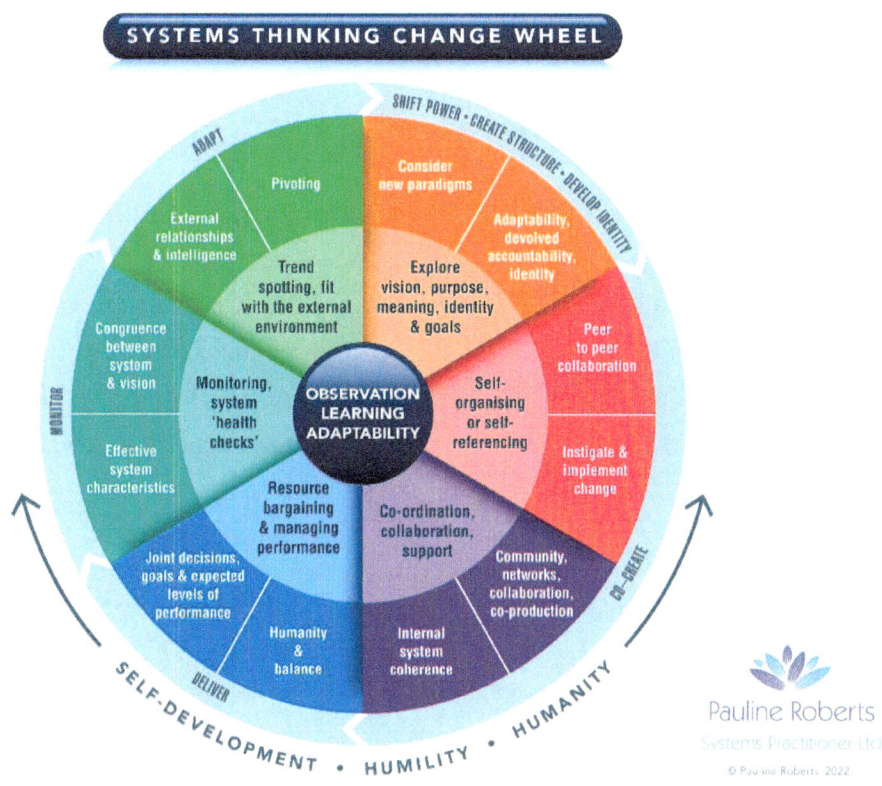

Figure 1: Systems Thinking Change Wheel

Self-organising or self-referencing (Pink)

Starting with the pink segment, which has been inspired by system 1, the primary operations of the VSM. The key area of focus to contemplate is self-organisation and/ or self-referencing. To what extent does this happen in the operational elements of your situation? Is it relevant? If not, why not? Should it be? Then consider the outer area of the pink segment. Can peer-to-peer collaborations support the level of self-organisation and/ or self-referencing that you think is appropriate in your situation? This outer area also prompts you to consider instigating and implementing change. Do people in the situation know how to instigate and make a change? In my experience, there is often an assumption that they do. They often do not. They have an idea but find it difficult to move it forward because no one has ever taught them how.

Coordination, collaboration, support (Purple)

The second segment to contemplate is the purple segment, which is inspired by system 2 coordination of the VSM. The inner area of the segment tells us that coordination, collaboration and support are important things to consider. The outer area prompts us to go further and consider what kind of community or networks might be useful to help coordination. How we collaborate and how we co-produce can be important. The other element we are prompted to consider here is system coherence.

Resource bargaining and managing performance (Blue)

Let's move on to the blue segment, which is inspired by system 3, delivery of the VSM. Here we are prompted to consider how resource bargaining and performance management occur, just as in the VSM. However, the outer area prompts us to also consider whether joint decisions, joint goals or agreed levels of performance would be beneficial and how we might bring humanity and balance back into the work.

Monitoring and system health checks (Turquoise)

The turquoise segment is inspired by system 3* monitoring of the VSM. Here I advocate for system health checks. I also think it pertinent to consider the congruence between the system and its vision. Sometimes the two are far from aligned. To support the system health checks, I advocate for exploring whether the system is exhibiting effective system characteristics.

Trendspotting, fit with the external environment (Green)

The green segment is inspired by system 4 intelligence of the VSM. Here we see in the inner area that trendspotting and fitting with the external environment might be important. The outer area tells us to consider our external relationships and our ability to pivot.

Explore vision, purpose, meaning, identity and goals (Orange)

The final segment is the orange one, inspired by system 5, governance of the VSM. Here, it is important to explore things like purposes, meaning, identity and goals. They do not have to be aligned, but there may be beneficial accommodations that can be made in the situation. Devolved accountability may be important to explore, as well as adaptability and identity. I also focus on considering new paradigms. Are you the one standing in the way of a shift?

Around the edge of the circle, you will see the areas segmented with grey arrows. These show which segments falls into co-creating, delivering, monitoring, adapting, shifting power, creating structure, and developing identity.

Across the bottom of the circle, personal development comes into play. Self-development, humility and humanity are important to remember and are the ethos of this approach.

Areas of focus

As already mentioned, the segments are inspired by areas in Stafford Beer's VSM, but in this part of my approach, remember that it is the traits of humanity, leadership, caring, empathy, consciousness, inner confidence, and wisdom that I focus on, rather than just the management outlined in the VSM.

This is not a blueprint to follow. They are things that may be important to consider. Context is exceptionally important and everything we do as systems thinking practitioners should be context specific.

The central elements of the approach

You will notice that the central elements of this approach are observation, learning and adaptability.

Observation

Observation is a critical and yet largely overlooked skill for a practitioner. Many people I have worked with can sense things about a situation. Deep inside they know what it is, yet often, they struggle to articulate it. This tends to prevent them from thinking about or suggesting improvements or alternatives that might serve them better. This can be true with observations about ourselves also. How do we recognise our own patterns and step into them to support ourselves to work with empathy and ethics?

I saw this phenomenon where people struggled to articulate what they were observing in a lot of the systems change work I did. It was something I worked on a lot with people, so it is inevitable that it became central to my Creating the Conditions for Change approach. I have developed a supplementary set of action cards which help people consider the patterns of system behaviour they see and what they might mean. They make that which is right in front of people and yet invisible become visible.

Learning

I have included learning as a central element of my approach. Every section of the wheel should include at least double-loop learning and preferably triple-loop learning. Observing and learning for yourself, learning together as a group, and learning to reflect on your own reflections, scrutinising and critiquing your own framing and perspectives to open up further opportunities is key. This can be built as a habit into the very heart of how you work, should you so wish. However, as I write, an update to this work is already in progress. This element is changing to become self-development . The two are not necessarily the same and in my opinion, it is self-development that is an even more crucial element of this approach overall. It is where I start and what I focus on throughout.

Adaptability

Being adaptive to the external environment is the key to survival. The whole of this approach intends to support being adaptive, whatever you are applying it to, from an individual, a team, a service, an organisation or across multiple organisations. Without being adaptive over time, you are not likely to survive and therefore, it was important for me to include this as a central element.

Now, let's consider each of these six areas of focus in turn in more depth.

1. Self-organising/ self-referencing

Getting the right balance of autonomy

For individuals and teams, there is a very fine balance between giving autonomy and maintaining the cohesion of your organisation, team or service. I use this idea to look at how appropriate self-organisation and/ or self-referencing might be used to support the autonomy of the individuals and yet maintain cohesion in their situation. I consider how much management control is optimum and I use the concept of self-referencing to consider the extent to which people know themselves and understand their own frames of reference and how that impacts both them and the work. I consider autonomy as a way of supporting requisite variety, which enables people to appropriately manage the complexity they have to deal with daily.

I saw this dilemma play out in the NHS organisation that had issues with receiving products into the department. To what extent would self-organisation or self-referencing have been appropriate in that situation? It is an interesting question to ponder. Nowadays, self-organisation is often talked about as if it is the ideal to aspire to. I do not necessarily agree. In the situation I recounted, self-organisation would have been a step too far, particularly because the organisation was so highly regulated.

Self-referencing is probably closer to what I see occurring most often in my work and it is a more realistic aspiration. In your work, to what extent are people able to self-reference? Do they know what it is? Do you know what your frames of reference are? Are people able to self-reference well and step into their frames of reference and change them, if required? What effect does that have? Does it bring new insights into their work? Does it enable them to work well with the level of autonomy they have been given? Do they need more autonomy? Or less? There are lots of questions to ponder here.

Working effectively together – in teams and across teams

In my commissioning manager roles, I certainly found that working across teams was as important as working well within my own team. If we did not work effectively across the team and organisational boundaries, the work did not progress. The same was true of working across team boundaries in the pharmaceutical laboratories. I believe that silos are not always a bad thing, but it is always a good idea to have a pathway between them, to make each side accessible when required.

What I saw in some teams was that different silos did not communicate well with each other. As a result, the teams struggled to cooperate and coordinate work effectively. When doing work reviewing an NHS community paediatrics service, I met two teams who worked on the periphery of the service. They were not directly involved but were close enough for me to be interested in the way they worked. They often defaulted to competing rather than collaborating. They struggled to make meaning of each other's behaviours and requests. It caused untold issues in the flow of the work and a lot of people's time was spent dealing with it day in and day out.

Yet in general, I have found that most teams collaborate well and often become stronger because of it. Of course, collaboration is not always appropriate, but in some cases, it is. Collaborating is not easy. It requires that you are honest with each other, so you can build up trust. That means, as an individual, you need to be comfortable enough with yourself to trust others and be vulnerable, if required. This is the element of human development in the approach that is needed to evolve our inner wisdom and ethics.

Other important things to consider in this area of focus are how people build a sense of community and collaboration between teams and with their wider partners or communities. That is, of course, if a sense of community is what is required and appropriate.

Identifying opportunities for innovation

This involves exploring and exploiting opportunities for innovation. People do not always know how to exploit opportunities that are right in front of them, because no one has taught them how. Opportunities pass by because people do not know how to reach out, grab them and make the most of them. Would you or your team know how to identify and exploit an opportunity that presented itself? Or would it just fly on by?

Reciprocation

Reciprocation has been an important concept to me in all of my work to date. At the highest level, it is possible to purposefully create reciprocation strategies or agreements between teams in one organisation, between teams in different organisations, or between whole organisations. I saw examples of this reciprocation in the Transfer of Care Protocol work between neighbouring hospitals and the urgent care reciprocal agreements made across regions. It is quite possible to build these strategies into policy documents, protocols etc. and actively enable them if you want and need to.

Imagine making reciprocation the norm. Why not? It is too radical an idea? Do you all have different targets and purposes? Who is going to be brave enough to start working differently? What can you agree in advance that would make life easier when times get tough? Are there any reciprocation strategies that both sides can live with? They may not meet everyone's needs all of the time, but they could at least be the best possible fit, acknowledging that some compromise will always be required and someone or something, somewhere might need to lose out a little.

Relationships

I am sure you will have picked up on this already. Purposefully building relationships, especially with teams outside of your immediate team, is frequently an enabler in creating the conditions for change. Do not perceive relationships as something that are secondary or that happen automatically. You have to actively work at building relationships. How about considering those you normally fight with and focusing on changing the nature of those relationships? It might take one side to wave a white flag to get the ball rolling, but it is not impossible. Talking about each other's strengths and where you can help each other can be a great way forward. When relationships are nurtured, I have seen people and/ or teams form a different identity. In the laboratories, we went from work colleagues to the family. It was a much more supportive and collaborative framing.

Reflective conversations

Engaging in reflective conversations is crucial. How often do you give yourself even a few minutes to engage in a reflective conversation with your teammates? It can help you to positively challenge ideas and it can also create opportunities to consider people's feelings, including your own. Think of the discharge person I found crying in an office. If you are in a situation that is generally struggling, everyone is likely feeling some degree of tiredness, fear or anxiety and they are probably overwhelmed.

Acknowledge these feelings and consider actively coaching and supporting each other, informally. We are often told that allowing vulnerability and learning together can be effective, so why do we not engage in it more often?

Take your time

One word of warning I give people is to not go too fast or put unreasonable expectations on each other. It often helps to keep things realistic. That said, I do encourage people to push outside of their emotional comfort zone so that new norms can have a chance of forming. I also remind people to be supportive of others who are trying to do the same. Keeping it simple, being authentic, maintaining your integrity and actively engaging in self-referencing sounds easy but they are things that can be quite hard to achieve. You may have to be very honest with yourself along the way and I have found that this can be quite difficult. Indeed, the self-reflection and self-development I advocate for may, at times, need to be a private activity.

Power

When considering self-reflection and reciprocation, I encourage people to also consider the notion of power. Check yourself. Are you creating any boundaries to defend or preserve yourself or your power base? Letting go of some of your power so that you can work well with those around you can give you greater capacity to create something different or new. Releasing power is not always easy, though. It can make you feel vulnerable, which might be why people cling to it so tightly. This is where trust comes in. There must be sufficient trust to allow vulnerability. Letting go of power can be an effective enabler to create the conditions for change, although it is not easy to achieve in practice and you will need to make your own decisions about how to accomplish it in your context.

Purpose

I also prompt people to consider purpose. What is the purpose of the team, service, or organisation in which you work and your purpose? Are they aligned? If they are not, try and work out why. Can that be reconciled? If so, how? And how might this be raised with management so that those purposes can be aligned more closely if you need them to be? I will stress, 'If you need them to be'. It is feasible to have different purposes, and in some cases it is inevitable. Yet, sometimes, when purposes are at odds with each other, it can cause upset and/ or demotivation. I saw a huge misalignment of purpose in the social work teams I visited. Austerity cuts are certainly doing a good job of pulling individuals away from their professional purposes for doing the work. The results I have seen so far have upset and demoralised people.

Prototyping

As a collaborative of people and/ or teams, you can explore, experiment, fail, and learn together. Small-scale prototyping can help this process, although this is a difficult concept to embed in some organisations, such as the NHS due to the current dependency on pilots and evidence-based approaches. I do encourage people to explore together to find out what obstructs, disrupts, delays or diverts their work. I encourage them to disturb things in positive ways. It is important, though that people know how to try things out. This is a skill I have found repeatedly lacking and as such, it is a key skill for consideration.

Supporting skills and behaviours

What skills and/ or behaviours can support this area of focus? In my experience, it has been the ability to coach and support one another. Being able to orchestrate our inner selves is also critical. Alongside that, developing our receptiveness to the thoughts and suggestions of others is key. Being an innovator is useful and within that, I would include the ability to think critically, build up a contextual understanding of situations and be accountable for your actions. There were no heroes in any of my systems thinking work, only contributors and/ or supporters.

2. Coordination, collaboration and support

Coordination

People, teams, services and organisations need mechanisms that coordinate and support their operational activities. This is just like in the VSM. These mechanisms are most effective when they are not overburdening top-down controls. This is an important area for consideration and it is very often overlooked. It was especially evident in my work with social workers, where they had a very scant supporting infrastructure and were becoming individually swamped every day, as a result of having to perform the same simple problem-solving tasks over and over again. It took an inordinate length of time. Some of that effort could easily have been reduced with computer systems and other processes to support, rather than hinder them. The complexity, instead, fell on the shoulders of the people involved in the work and it made them crumble under the weight of it.

It can be highly detrimental to your work if you do not explicitly consider how things will be coordinated effectively and just leave things to fall into place automatically. I can tell you that they rarely do. I call these coordinating mechanisms the invisible glue in organisations. They are the things that hold everything together in a coherent way, even the invisible patterns of behaviour. Ignore these things at your peril. Get them right and they can significantly enhance your capacity and capability, often at little or no cost. Do not underestimate the value that getting this element right can bring.

Relationship enablers and interaction channels

Not only will you need to create and/or implement standard things like protocols, rules, guidance, schedules, etc - you may also need to give attention to generating and sharing information freely, building connections, communities and networks and working collaboratively. Loops of mutual influence can be particularly effective. It is harder than it sounds, but it can be done. It just takes a little bit of persistence.

Extremely important is something I call relationship-enablers. These are the things you put in place and/ or the mindset you adopt that supports the dynamic connectedness in your situation. Relationship enablers are exactly how they sound. They are things that enable relationships. This can be as simple as a clause in a joint protocol that considers something from more than one point of view to something more elaborate, like a process for discussing and agreeing on difficult decisions between a number of stakeholders. They are the things that give permission for the collaboration to occur. They can help to enable proactive dialogue, negotiation and agreements and enable relationships in the longer term.

The other extremely important thing here is what I call interaction channels to enable collaboration. They might be mechanisms created to enable reflective conversations. Do you ever have a joint meeting with another team, department, or organisation specifically to reflect and learn from the work you do? Do you discuss problems and issues and seek to implement improvements together? Do you have a culture of positive challenge and learning? You can develop your internal structures so that people have enough freedom to enable collaborative working.

Shadowing another team, for example, should not be seen as wasting time, but as a valuable interaction channel and relationship enabler that can open up support for ongoing collaboration and learning. Do your current structures allow for interaction, collaboration and smaller teams to work together effectively? Particularly across boundaries? Or is there too much interference and control from above? More control does not necessarily mean better results and in some cases, it can make things considerably worse. Remember the flight across the bicycle handlebars?

At all scales in your situation, you can develop collaborative strategies and contracts (formal and informal) that enable longer-term collaboration. These are all relationship enablers and negotiating them via an interaction channel can support you to work effectively.

Collaboration and co-production

One of your collaboration strategies might be co-production. But if yours is nothing more than a single workshop with no further follow-up, then I would not class it as co-production. Co-production should be an ongoing process of collaboration, rather than a one-off activity. See it as working together long term and build it into your working routine until it becomes a habit.

Sharing stories

Share stories, even the bad ones. Particularly the bad ones. Sharing a story of when something went wrong is not something to be ashamed of. If done well, it can be a key way to learn and should be encouraged. Be open. Talk a lot. Share a lot. Get out from behind your computer screens and go and look at what is happening in reality. Do not rely only on figures on a computer. They often miss the real point. Go out and experience how things happen in context. Look for patterns of recurring system behaviour. Do the system behaviours need to change, or do they need more encouragement?

Feedback loops

Another important part of this element is enabling feedback loops and checking they are working. Feedback loops are an important element of the VSM and they are effective in helping to create the conditions for change.

Consider the process that occurs when a message is shared with another party. It is important that the message is received and interpreted as it was intended, and some kind of action is taken, as intended. Feedback from that action needs to be fed back into the system and further actions taken in response. Often, messages are lost or misunderstood.

When you have a message for another team or group of people, how do you know that they will hear your message? How do you know that the message will be interpreted as you want it to be interpreted? How do you know they will respond to it appropriately? Will the action taken be as you expected? And how will you know that the action has been effective? These are all very important parts of a feedback loop to consider.

Remember to also create and share information that is capable of bringing new life to your situation, rather than creating and sharing information that just confirms what already is.

Learning and growing

Learning and growing is a huge part of this area of focus. Building supporting mechanisms to enable learning is vital. This does not have to be formal mechanisms. Encouraging dialogue and sharing is often enough to motivate people to learn. Get the feedback loops established and you might well find that learning follows. They worked excellently for us in the laboratories.

Supporting skills and behaviours

What skills and/ or behaviours can support this area of focus? It can help to develop community and build networks if people are willing to enter into a relationship of mutual trust and respect. That can take transparency and reciprocity. Facilitation skills can also be useful, especially in the early days of bringing people together or working in different ways. If you want to share, storytelling is very powerful. How many valuable things happen every day that people do not record and then are lost forever?

Of course, some people are natural networkers and orchestrators of change. Use their skills wisely.

3. Day-to-day delivery

In the VSM, this area of focus is about managing the day-to-day delivery of the operations. Part of that is to bargain for resources and manage performance. This is a standard area of focus in work situations. One way to do it effectively is by a process of joint decisions about what resources are required and provided and what level of performance is considered appropriate for that level of resource. We did this really well when we worked in the laboratories. At the time, I did not appreciate it half as much as I should have. In my version of this area of focus, I encourage my clients to consider bringing humanity back into the work. An appropriate balance of work that does not cause burnout is common sense. Burnt-out people being pushed to do ever more is no good for anyone.

Involve people in decision making, where possible and feasible

This can be quite a controversial point and not always appropriate. We cannot always involve everyone in decision-making. That would be totally inappropriate in many circumstances. However, I do ask people to consider whether those who could be easily and feasibly included in decision-making, have been. If people have been involved in goal setting in particular, it can prevent them from feeling coerced. It is especially important to remember that many people like their own professional values reflected in the work they do. This is a reciprocal offering that can bring people on board with certain goals, and they may give something in return, like dedication or insights. If my values are not reflected in the work I am doing, there is no point in me being there. I move on, very quickly. Meaningful work, that aligns with people's values and indeed, their identity, can be a powerful motivator and help to create the conditions for change.

Trust

In our laboratory teams, we trusted each other. In commissioning, we trusted each other. In the place-based systems change work, we trusted each other. Working hand in hand with others often takes trust. That is not to say that you cannot make change without trust. Many people do and are very successful at it, particularly consultants who are hired to go into an organisation to make a quick change. However, trust can help with longer-term relationships, enabling you to nurture those relationships over time. If you are working with people long-term, a lack of trust may gradually erode the conditions that support effective change.

It is important to trust without micro-managing. The autonomy gifted to people can see accountability gifted in return. If I had tried to micro-manage my teams in the laboratories or pharmacy production, I am very sure they would have told me where to go, in no uncertain terms. Especially the people in the laboratories. Remember that most were headstrong Geordies! Remaining hands-off can have its advantages, although you do need to gauge when this is appropriate.

Peer-to-peer support

Another option is allowing people to have their peer-to-peer performance meetings, just like we did in the laboratories. We held each other to account. We also encouraged each other to share ideas that would help the teams who were falling behind. It is a simple thing and yet can be so effective because people are reciprocating with each other, which helps the relationships to develop. If you have meetings in a peer-to-peer setting, a way to prevent any single person dominating is to have a rolling host for the meetings, so no one assumes ultimate power or control.

Infectious behaviours

When you are responsible for the everyday delivery of something, sometimes all it takes to inspire people to make change is to behave in a certain way. Model the type of behaviours that will make your situation flourish. I have seen this in the NHS offices when I was a commissioning manager. Someone would deal with a situation in the office or on the phone really well and the next thing, everyone was copying that style, having seen that it worked well. Then, someone would do something else that worked really well, and people would try that out for themselves.

I learnt how to be a manager and leader by watching other people and seeing what worked for them. When I worked on place-based systems change I found it important to model the behaviours that we expected participants in the workshops to exhibit. Behaviours are infectious. After all, what other opportunities are there to get our benchmarks for empathetic and ethical work? Especially when our governments and media are pumping out anything other than empathetic and ethical messaging.

Conflict

If there is conflict, and there inevitably will be, you do not necessarily need to avoid it. Conflict can often be a sign that there is an unrealised opportunity afoot. Hold deeper exploratory conversations instead. It is the same with confusion and disruption. They can be sure signs that an opportunity is hiding in plain sight.

Effectiveness

One key thing to bring to your attention about day-to-day delivery is that focusing on efficiency only and not effectiveness can be a false economy. In my work, I have rarely focused on gaining efficiencies. I have focused on effectiveness and the money and efficiency took care of themselves. Effectiveness can bring about efficiencies you never thought of, so do not focus too narrowly on financial savings all the time.

Appraising for appropriate behaviours

Appraisals. They are awful, aren't they? I hate them. I find them forced and formal and rarely reflective of anything to do with me or my learning. But, how else do you encourage the right habits to form in your teams, services or organisations? You could experiment with developing ways of appraising people that praise things like critical thinking, sharing, collaborating, encouraging others to empower themselves, and coaching and supporting peers. These can nurture competence, confidence and adaptability.

This need not be done by the old-fashioned formal appraisal format, either. Any general recognition, as long as it is genuine, can be effective. I remember doing an appraisal for a laboratory team member who thought he was in trouble because of some things that had happened. I started by praising him for working closely with another team member who had been struggling. He had shown him how to make products and how to manoeuvre around the laboratories a little less clumsily. He was patient and empathetic. He did it very unassumingly when he thought no one was watching. I was watching, quietly, from the sidelines. That appraisal went from what could have been a very tense session, to one where that member of staff became my number two for training. I rewarded him for his initiative. I gave him autonomy to co-design a fun and interactive training programme for laboratory staff with me and he seemed to love it. We both had great fun with it. I was actively encouraging the leadership habits he had already demonstrated. All I was doing was letting him know how valuable they were.

Responding to corporate instructions

Make sure any instructions and corporate standards are incorporated into the daily work in a timely way. This is also part of the VSM. They cannot and should not be ignored and there should be ways to embed them quickly and easily into daily practices. Give some thought to how this can be done. Do you have a culture of ignoring new corporate instructions? Or embedding them so slowly that they are almost out of date by the time they become common practice? Yes? Then there is an opportunity for you to strengthen both your mechanisms for dissemination and your response to new instructions.

This becomes critical when it is linked to the requirements of the future. There may be times when you need to make changes quickly. Make sure you have the structures, the dynamics and the relationships in place to allow this to happen. If you cannot change quickly enough when needed, you may find your team or your wider service or organisation becomes obsolete.

Supporting skills and behaviours

What skills and/ or behaviours can support managing the day-to-day delivery of the operations? Having skills in destroying, removing or temporarily dissolving barriers can be critical. My director in commissioning was a talented destroyer of barriers, which I found really motivating and I believe many of my colleagues did also.

Of course, this area of focus is about bargaining for resources and agreeing on performance, so being a good negotiator comes in handy. If you are making change in your own department or service, skills in spotting patterns of system behaviours in your situation might also be useful.

Knowing how to develop different enabling structures for changes you want to make is also important. Do you know how to configure your teams so that they can thrive in complexity and in times when there is no set plan for what happens next? What happens if you remove one significant person from your team? McChrystal, in his book *Team of Teams*, found that having a lack of traditional hierarchy meant that there was no internal anarchy by the removal of significant individuals. The hierarchy is maintained but in a different way. I believe that there should be a combination of management and teamwork and dare I say it, if people want to quit, let them. Teams are effective when they work as a coordinated whole, not when one person dominates.

It almost goes without saying that being able to communicate well and encourage transparent exchanges of information is a worthwhile skill. However, it is easy to forget the effort required for transparent information exchanges. If teams produce clear information, then the hierarchy can be satisfied from a distance. After all, those closest to the problematic situation can generally offer nuanced insights that enable decisive action.

Enabling, rather than directing has become a much talked about leadership skill of late. It requires clear, unambiguous and consistent messaging. We also need to keep a check on our behaviours.

I have also found the advice given in Gareth Morgan's book, *Riding the Waves of Change* valuable. It was written in the 1980s but remains relevant today. It is interesting to consider how difficult it can be for managers to be both technical specialists and people managers. This is something to keep in mind.

Conflict management and modelling successful personal interactions comes up repeatedly in my work as areas of skill development in this area of focus. It is skills like these that link to our inner development and how we grow and use our wisdom. There is much more work to do here to fully step into a new paradigm and I wonder how many more years it will be before we truly arrive there.

4. Monitoring and system 'health checks'

More often than not, organisations use performance indicators to ascertain how well they are doing. You may never be able to get rid of these and I would not advocate for doing so. I know for sure that performance indicators were seen as very important by every organisation I have worked for. Yet they will not tell you how healthy your situation is on the ground. After all, we can make our performance indicators say anything we want them to, if we try. There is an additional activity we can undertake, which is monitoring. I was inspired to make monitoring central to my work. I focus on checking if effective system characteristics are present and whether there is congruence between what people say their vision is and what they are actually doing.

To be clear here, I do not advocate for a senior manager doing the monitoring. That can make teams feel watched or spied upon. I also do not necessarily advocate for external evaluation. I feel that peer-to-peer monitoring can be used to build supportive and helpful relationships, as we did in the laboratories.

Monitoring for effective system characteristics

Do you routinely check if your structures are facilitating the work on the ground, rather than interfering with it? This is one of the key things I look for as a consultant and when I am working internally in an organisation. I might explore complaints and compliments and consider what they are telling me. More often than not, I go and have a look around. I watch and listen and absorb what is happening. I sit in waiting rooms and see how people are being dealt with. I go out on rounds with staff and sit in their offices. I watch the work happening in its context. That way, people cannot tell me only what they think I want to hear.

If a team, service, or organisation appears to be suffering, I explore whether they are lacking information about themselves. Have they lost clarity about what or who they are? Have they got troubled relationships? Are they ignoring those with valuable insights? You can do something about all of these things. Finding out how things are working operationally through informal channels can be a very valuable activity and definitely worth the time. As I mentioned though, be wise about how you do it. No one likes to feel watched.

Monitor for the ability to flex, adapt, pivot, enable change and respond to the changing environment. We used to do tabletop simulations in the NHS for urgent care. They were hilarious. Absolutely nothing went smoothly. Sorry everyone, but back then, we were rubbish at it. It gave us insights into our ability to flex and respond though.

It is important not to just look at things when they are at the point of crisis. I encourage my clients to enact system health checks or early warning systems to indicate the health of a situation. These have been useful in system change work. If you know your situation is starting to get sick, it can be much better to react when it has a cold, rather than when it is in the throes of pneumonia.

Congruence between vision and actions

I also encourage people to check for congruence between their own, team, service, department, organisation or place's vision and the behaviour that is evident in the situation. I focus on the people, what they are doing and how they are doing it. Are they happy and fulfilled in their work? This is the element of bringing humanity into the approach that I advocate for. Of course, you are not always going to have happy members of staff but if you have consistently high turnover and people are unhappy most of the time, there is clearly an issue.

A dead giveaway that there is a lack of congruence is when you find a lovely glossy brochure, usually written by consultants, that does not reflect the reality before your eyes. Promoting a vision of the ideal is not a bad thing and is often expected, but sometimes it is not helpful. No one is likely to air their dirty washing in public but internally, if something is not working, then face it. You cannot improve it if you do not admit it and face it, even if it is painful.

Supporting skills and behaviours

What skills and behaviours can support monitoring? Being a good system health check monitor . Are you able to spot patterns of system behaviour, as in the last section? Can you really observe what you are seeing and make sense of it? These skills are crucial to monitor your situation effectively or you just end up relying on what people tell you and that can very often be incorrect. It might even have a perverse motivation sitting behind it. Learn to see the symptoms at an early stage before they spiral out of control.

5. Trendspotting and fitting with the external environment

Exploring the interface between the situation and the wider context is another important area. We need to identify future emerging trends and bring that external information into our situations and share it to help develop structures and practices that will be fit for the future. It can be very useful to scan the environment for new models of doing things and bring that insight into your team to encourage innovation.

You can evaluate what you are currently doing to prevent yourself from maintaining a focus on activities that will not be required in the future. I encourage my clients to check that there is an actual need for what they are doing. I get them to link it to their purpose. It is surprising how many teams or services just keep on doing because they always have. There is an opportunity for my clients to take active steps to make sure the things they do are the things that will be required going forward. They just have to want to consider it. Will you still be relevant in the future? You might need to stop doing certain things. Loss may be necessary to create something new. This was the function that failed in our pharmaceutical laboratories. No matter how fast we went, the environmental demands were faster than us. We did not have a quick enough way to respond to them and we crumbled.

If you decide that change is necessary to align with future trends and external requirements, there is an opportunity to work proactively with operational managers to discuss it. Our senior manager in the laboratories did this. We set up our internal operations to cope with the even greater demands that we knew were coming. The senior manager worked one-to-one with us so that we could all do our best to adapt. Not everything works out every time, though. In that case, our rate of change was not quite quick enough and we, unfortunately, plummeted into the abyss as a result.

Supporting skills and behaviours

What skills and/ or behaviours can support this area of focus? Identifying trends in your environment that you might want to respond to is crucial here. If you cannot spot them, they can be a danger. Also, if you do not know how to work with internal colleagues so that you can adapt and respond to any new trend you want to adopt, you are not going to be able to change quickly enough.

Being able to spot complementarity in a situation can also be valuable, particularly when developing strategies based on structural couplings. Structural coupling is when something interacts with its environment in a way that both the entity and the environment change each other. The idea of structural coupling is hugely unexplored territory, just waiting to be discovered more explicitly in business. I have not personally come across anyone in business yet, outside of systems thinking practitioners, who deliberately engage with this type of thinking and actively seek to understand and use structural couplings to their benefit. It can be especially helpful if you are in the area of health and care, where there are many potential areas of complementarity with the partners around you.

6. Governance, power, structures and identity

Different visions and goals

Different players in a situation often have unrelated strategic visions and goals. This can cause people working across boundaries to get confused about their purpose and identity. They can easily become disorientated and demoralised as a result. It is fine, however, for different organisations, teams, and individuals to have different goals, vision and identities. In fact, it is likely to be detrimental if they do not. There is, however, likely to be some common overlapping element holding them together. It can be useful to explore what this might be so that you can utilise that information to your advantage. You may find that it is your humanity itself that binds you together and this is an area where I feel we could step into a new paradigm in time.

Power and autonomy

I mentioned power and autonomy in a previous section. This focus area relates to having a function that checks how you are governing your operations and what balance of autonomy and cohesion you have and who holds the power in your structures. Nowadays, there is a lot of recognition for shifting power, so that teams have a good balance of autonomy. Exploring where the power currently sits can be quite revelatory. The social workers I engaged with seemed to have little power in a situation where I would have thought that having much more power, particularly in decision-making, would have been beneficial.

In some situations, particularly in systems change, people might aim to have a network of influence in their working environments, rather than a strongly dominant chain of command. These networks of influence are particularly important in health and care environments also, where influence is especially relevant.

To support the networks, you might want to develop internal policies that include strategies for sharing, collaborating and enabling others at a more strategic level. I do not see these very often, but they are a possibility to consider.

I would like to go further than this and suggest that the habits of effective collaboration and relationship building nurture both us and our workplaces and can take us to a different place in our lives, not just our work.

Supporting skills and behaviours

What skills and behaviours can support this area of focus? Do you find it easy to nurture competence and adaptability? Can you help others to explore purpose? Are you able to develop structures that alleviate fear and support devolved decision-making? These are all key skills here. Do you feel comfortable sharing and enabling? Are your communications clear and consistent? Do you feel comfortable enough with yourself that you are able to trust others? Are you a good influencer by display of your ethical habits and do you embrace the deep wisdom of others? Do you extinguish inappropriate selfishness by modelling a better way? Your behaviours can be infectious so use them wisely.

Exploring and enabling systems change

When I was working on systems change with a variety of different groups, I realised that it required some more strongly targeted considerations, particularly with regards to empathy and the inner confidence of the individuals involved, which are captured in the infographic below.

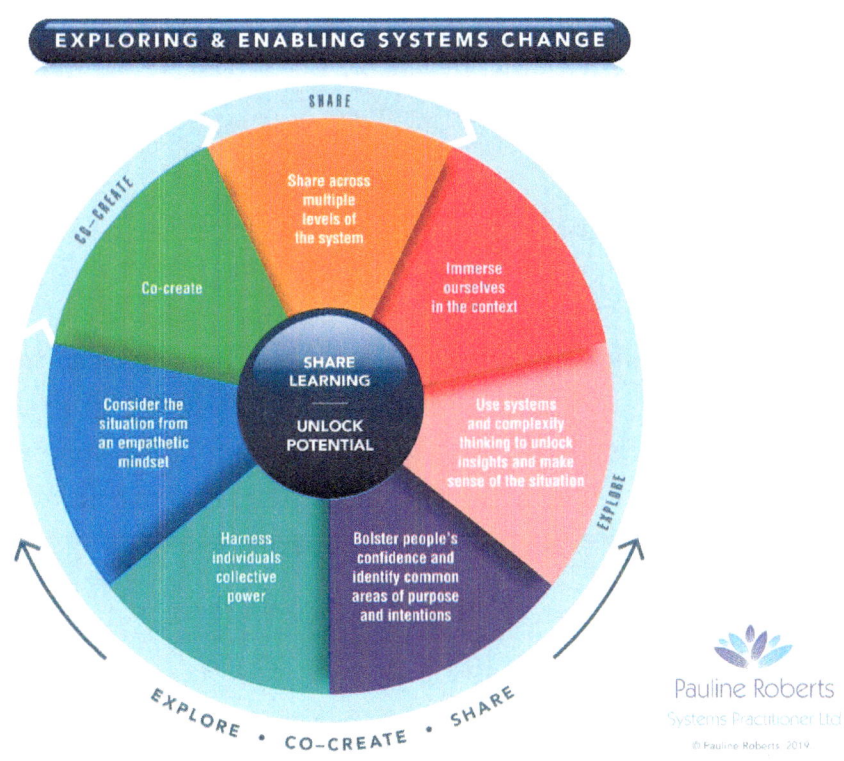

Figure 2: Exploring and Enabling Systems Change

In enacting this approach, there is a requirement to support and encourage people as they bolster their inner confidence. Most people I have worked with needed a safe space in which to learn. Then, working together, individuals became better equipped to harness their collective power to create change. Do not underestimate how easy it is for people to lose sight of their self-worth, which then erodes their inner confidence. It is important that they gain sight of themselves again and realise that they have valuable gifts to share.

Empathy

I have mentioned that an essential element of my approach has been to consider the situation from the mindset of empathy. This element did not come easily to me and in some cases, still doesn't. Only when I can understand the situation from the perspectives of others can I really understand it and I am aware of my limitations. With the best will in the world and with all of the materials to support me, I am always going to have huge blind spots. I can never know what it is like for all of my clients. I rely on them telling me and we need to create the right conditions for the trust to build quickly, so that can happen.

Learning, leadership and love

All things considered, a large element of this approach is about learning, leadership and love. We, as individuals, are constantly learning. We can transform situations when we flip the underlying emotion of the situation to love. In doing so, we demonstrate our enlightened, conscious leadership. If we are fortunate, this infects others who inspire themselves to select more positive framings that open up additional options for development, improvement and change.

Working at multiple scales

When we share and make changes at multiple scales in our situations at the same time, there is a potential for powerful change, even when the actions are small. This was the case in my hospital discharge work, and I will never forget it. We worked at the operational, tactical and strategic levels all at the same time. The results took me by surprise. Therefore, my approach is designed to be used at different scales, just as the VSM is. I even use it annually on myself for personal development purposes.

Part 3: The Systems Thinking Practitioner's Journey

Pauline Roberts

Chapter 6: The practitioner's journey – the invisible practitioner

This is where I am now. With an approach of my own to add to the already established systems thinking approaches that I use. On my journey so far, there have been recurring themes that I am now going to share with you. They are things that I get asked about by other systems thinking practitioners most often, particularly those who are just starting out on their journey. They are things that some practitioners encounter but often without the knowledge that others contend with the same challenges. They are the things that are much less talked about or documented and yet they can be quite significant aspects of the journey. I coach a lot of people around these topics and find that they are the things that can make people want to give up because their journey on the bridge feels too hard.

It is my hope that sharing my own experiences will make other practitioners reading this feel a little less alone. All journeys have rabbit holes, just like the one I went down. They have dark corners and deep pits full of gruesome insects and stagnant water. They also have moments of enlightening delight and sheer joy. I believe that if, as practitioners, we can share and learn from our unpredictable journeys through the dark muddy warrens and pools of stagnant water, then we might just be able to help others as they, too, feel like the only person who has fallen headfirst down a dark gaping hole.

The invisibility cloak

'Pauline, it's like everything I do is invisible. Like I am invisible! I am trying so hard but it's like I don't exist. No one recognises what I have had to do to get the work this far.' The coaching session was a tough one. My client's shoulders were slumped, their head pushed downwards and forwards, and I could see disillusionment and confusion on their faces. They were a very competent and capable practitioner, making great progress towards systems change. They and their colleagues had dealt with difficult relationships, brought people together into effective communities and were strides ahead of others in their understanding of systems thinking. But they felt invisible, and the story was familiar. Not only had I felt this way myself at times, but I had many colleagues and friends who had also expressed feeling invisible when putting systems thinking into practice.

What is this invisibility cloak that systems thinking practitioners wear? Is it something everyone wears when going about their daily work? Or is it specific to systems thinking practitioners? Clearly, I cannot speak for other professions but when it comes to putting systems thinking into practice, I believe invisibility is a common feeling.

I was contemplating the feeling of invisibility, and what it really meant to me back in 2021 when I was watching the series, *Manhunt* on ITV Player, for the third time. Yes, the third time! Manhunt is a UK ITV drama, with the actor Martin Clunes playing the lead role. There were two series. The first three-part dramatisation was about the killing of a young French student called Amelie de la Grange in 2004 in London. Detective Chief Inspector Colin Sutton led a manhunt that led to the arrest of a man called Levi Bellfield, who was subsequently found guilty of two other shocking murders and one attempted murder.

The second series, called *The Night Stalker* saw Colin Sutton drafted in to solve the case of Delroy Grant, a predatory sex attacker who would target older people in their homes, in London. Both cases were shocking in themselves, but what struck me was what Colin Sutton had to contend with in the dramatisation, on a day-to-day basis to be effective in his job. I saw lots of links between the challenges he faced and the challenges invisible practitioners face. I saw skills in his character's work that I often saw in the work of practitioners. The more I watched, the more insights were revealed. I watched it again a year later and I am sure I will watch it again. But what similarities did I see?

Firstly, it is pertinent to make clear that despite popular belief, systems thinking practitioners are not all business consultants who come into an organisation with fancy approaches and sprints to tell you what to do. They might not be the confident outsiders trying to wow you to get themselves more business. They are very often the ones who work inside of your organisation on a daily basis, overcoming very similar barriers to those Colin Sutton's character had to overcome, particularly in the first series about Levi Bellfield. I should say at this point that the programme was a dramatisation and I am talking about what was portrayed in the programme here, not the real work of those involved in the situation.

In the programme, Colin Sutton's character had the ability to zoom into details and check them out from a human perspective, rather than taking a 'computer says' perspective. This is a powerful skill for a practitioner. Many of us live and breathe our work and we are not looking for an easy way or a computer to tell us what to do. We will very often seek to step into the shoes of others and walk around in them, seeing the world through their eyes as best we can. I saw Colin Sutton's character working through what he would do if he was a killer who had the phone, keys and other items from a person they had just killed. How would a killer dispose of them? It was this 'what would a person do' touch that led the team to find the victim's possessions in a nearby river. Of course, practitioners are not generally looking to solve a murder, but they might be using a similar process of investigation to explore the situation they are engaging with.

I, for one, go through aspects of a scenario and try to fully experience what is going on for myself. I do not cut corners and this human touch, whilst painstaking at times, can open up a world of insights. Many practitioners will be the same and as such, will have developed exceptional observational skills. Some are often able to observe with several different lenses over their eyes and hold several versions of reality in their mind at the same time. This is one of our invisible skills. It can take many years to master these skills and yet they often reside firmly under our invisibility cloak.

Colin Sutton's character had a particular struggle to get past his doubters and hurdle those who were blocking him or were sceptical about his strategies. He allowed them to have their say and yet, at the same time, he never lost his focus. This completely resonated with me. As a practitioner it is common to have the doubters, blockers and sceptics knocking on your door the very instant you lift your head above the parapet, desperate to stop you in your tracks. But why do we put up with it? Why do we still keep trying to plough forwards? Is it not too hard? I can only speak for myself again here, but I do think this will resonate with many systems thinking practitioners. It is because I try and work authentically and ethically and I am determined that a positive difference can be made. If I believe in what I am doing, I can deal with doubters and sceptics. I can deal with those who try and block me because I know, at some point, the fruits of my labour will come to bear.

This kind of blocking can be par for the course in the world of systems thinking and many practitioners I know can either deal with it or learn coping mechanisms so that it does not get to them. These skills are not generally recognised by others. They are invisible and yet they can be a persistent challenge when enacting our practice.

Boatloads of courage

Some brave practitioners even stand up to game players and I have been known to stand up to a few myself. They call them out, no matter what the consequences are for themselves. They have courage. Boatloads of courage. But why? Won't that be detrimental for them, personally? Yes, it can be, but I do it because I believe in what I am doing and sometimes, when all else fails or when the situation is a serious one, the game players need calling out. I saw bravery in Colin Sutton's character. I saw him call out the blockers and express his frustrations. Sometimes, it is needed and as a practitioner, I am always prepared to stand up for what I believe in. Bravery is another part of the skillset that is often glaringly obvious and yet invisible at the same time.

Practitioners can be resented when casting fresh eyes on the past work and decisions of others, which was exactly what I saw Colin Sutton's character dealing with. Like him, practitioners learn how to effectively engage and work with, or in some cases around, those wearing their comfy slippers, who are fully committed to maintaining the status quo, which is usually desperately in need of change. It can make you feel like an outsider. Someone who is not part of the internal clique.

Keeping the faith

There are many times when I have had to stand alone, as people have tried to make fun of my work in an attempt to cast me and it out. I have had to deal with put-downs and belittling and I understand that many of these tactics might just be ploys to undermine and divert attention. I know many practitioners who have worked through this and it takes hard work and determination to keep going. It also takes great skill to not turn situations like these into conflict. Of course, there are many I have happily turned into conflict, but not generally in situations with my clients. Continuing to have faith in what you are doing, despite others not having that faith, is another one of our invisible skills.

Learning to deal with being undermined or ignored can feel like part of the work. There are times when I have expended much energy trying to get those on board who clearly do not want to come on board, or do not find it relevant to give their all to the cause. Despite this, I tend not to let it knock my confidence to ask questions that others dare not or do not want to. I saw this determination and courage in the client sat in front of me and I saw it in Colin Sutton's character in the programme. Confidence to ask the difficult questions and also knowing when to call it a day is another of our invisible skills.

Some practitioners I know, myself included, have learnt to come at things from a different angle when they are being ridiculed because people do not understand what they are doing. We are not perfect, though. We are people too and sometimes we fall into the trap of defending ourselves. We may have had to put up with bitterness, jealousy and general resentment from others for a long time and we may have taken the stance to not suffer fools any longer. More often than not though, practitioners seek to empathise with those trying to maintain control. There is usually an underlying reason for their stance. We understand that which is at stake for them and we can often help them to envision a new and less threatening reality. A reality which might even be easier for them. The empathetic stance is sometimes not an easy one, but it is one that a lot of practitioners are eagerly willing to take. It is another of our invisible skills.

We may, at times, have to work with people who take credit for our work or who only come on board as the results of our work are being seen, having not given us any slack in the formative, difficult stages of the work. I saw Colin Sutton's character dealing with senior managers standing in when it was time to be seen . These things sound ever so negative, but they do occur, and more often than not they happen in systems thinking work because we uncover that which has otherwise gone unseen. These challenges are real and often talked about by practitioners only in the confines of a safe space. I would like all practitioners and aspiring practitioners to know that this may be part of your journey at some stage and that is ok. You are not doing anything wrong. Others go through this too. Learning to deal with it can significantly develop your coping skills. The skills, of course, are part of our invisible skillset, hiding under our cloak, so you might have to come to terms with that.

Daring to be different

Colin Sutton's character was not afraid to go against the norm and try something different. This is another of a practitioner's invisible skills. I, for one, am prepared to try something different, even when I have absolutely no assurance that it will work. This is a giant leap of faith and sometimes, to be a successful practitioner, you need to encourage and support others to take the same leap of faith. I find it easier to genuinely do this if you have done it yourself at some stage.

Those who encourage a leap of faith without knowing what the consequences might feel like can tend to encourage recklessness. Anyone who knows me will know I hate phrases like 'speak truth to power'. This is not because I do not think we should speak truth to power. I think we should. However, I do not think we should encourage someone else to speak truth to power if we would not dare to do it ourselves or if we are encouraging someone to take a personal risk that both we and they do not fully understand. The consequence of speaking out or enacting work differently can often be a negative experience and people lose their livelihoods over such things. So do think before you encourage others and at the same time, do recognise your invisible skills – taking a leap of faith and daring to try something different.

The long game

Systems thinking practitioners often have particularly good skills in reframing to enable new opportunities to emerge and/or to release capacity in a system. They may accept that there are no quick fixes, but they will think through the best place to start, rather than giving up. A good practitioner may see the patterns in the situation and in people's behaviour which are derailing the work and they will look for other ways of doing things. Some spot when people are intentionally, or unintentionally, holding something in place to justify their own input and presence.

Practitioners will almost certainly challenge negative narratives which prevent a focus on what is important and may be willing to challenge the doubters or develop strategies to open up new perspectives. I saw Colin Sutton's character accept that his work may be painstaking and take a long time, but he dug in with determination and encouraged his team not to lose faith. He also challenged colleagues to open up their minds to new possibilities. More invisible skills.

Learning to learn

Most practitioners I know have learnt from those who came before them. They are willing and able to ask for help from others who have expertise that they do not. They often work with passion and purpose. They pick out the positives and stay focused. They keep their promises and may even add a personal touch. Taking responsibility and being convinced you can make a difference is part of the package. You may find that some practitioners are very serious about what they do and as a result, they are particularly thorough. They are also very prepared to change their mind if new information comes to light that brings a different perspective. They do their best to overcome their own dogmatism, which is a skill I rarely see in roles such as senior management. The place where it is needed so much.

Mistakes were made

It can be intimidating for some to have a practitioner in the camp. I have often come across people who think they are going to be exposed for past poor decision-making. An effective practitioner has the ability to accept, however, that mistakes in decision-making might have been made. Their intention is not to make people feel small or bad about themselves but to highlight the systemic nature of the situation and support people to understand that when things are not working well, it is rarely because of them personally, but because of a cascade of interlinked variables that have led the situation, often over a long period of time, to where it is now.

I remember working with a medical director and chief nurse once who seemed particularly nervous about my presence at first. After working with them for a while they realised that I was not there to expose them in any way, and they very quickly came to appreciate the support I brought to the situation. In fact, at the end of the work, I was asked to go and work for one of them to help them run their business. One of the things they told me at the end of the piece of work was, 'You never made us feel small, Pauline. Even though you knew we did not know any of this stuff.' Feel small, a chief nurse and medical director? You see, we all have our vulnerabilities and practitioners are acutely aware of this. It is part of our skillset to support others, not destroy them. We pick up on nuance and seek to understand people, rather than just looking at a situation in isolation from those who inhabit it. It is another of our invisible skills.

In the *Manhunt* series, I recognised the barriers, the hurdles, the doubters, the game players, the human errors, and the reliance on processes that did not work. I also recognised that what worked was a thorough understanding of people and the ability to think in a way that was not clouded by the lack of resources, poor procedures, human-imposed barriers and boundaries. The approach was steeped in empathy and common sense. The third time round, when I watched again to clarify what I thought I had seen, it was even more blindingly obvious.

Throughout all of our work, we have to prove ourselves as practitioners while manoeuvring hurdles on a regular basis. Our systems practice is an embodied habit that we have developed, sometimes over many years, and yet the refinement of those habits is generally invisible to all but ourselves. At the end of our pieces of work, there is no glory, just learning and then something else to focus on. The thoroughness, dedication, empathy, and insight can often go largely unseen. The invisibility cloak remains in place as we quietly slink away to our next piece of work.

Reflecting on my own personal journey of invisibility

Back in 2006, when I had my first real-life attempt at purposefully devising and using a hybrid systems thinking approach, I never thought I would be incorporating aspects of Soft Systems Methodology, Critical Systems Heuristics, System Dynamics and Viable System Modelling all under a cloak of invisibility. I tried my hand at rich pictures, systems maps, conceptual modelling, multiple cause diagramming and influence mapping. I made use of systems tools to open up perception, understand the culture and support complex decision-making. I identified levels of recursion, systems and sub-systems in my work situations. I engaged a number of multi-agency stakeholders using systems thinking approaches, identified how current policy had not been derived from some of the most appropriate information and I identified how previous ineffective planning had come about. I experimented with systems thinking language and significantly widened my views.

The personal learning and self-development were significant. I became very aware of the importance of perception and projection, unconscious bias, values and how I personally reacted to others. Whilst a massive learning curve for me and hugely insightful for the work I was undertaking, it was invisible to others. Imagine, coming that far and not being able to talk about it. The development of my work saw it turn from an ugly, brown caterpillar into a beautiful powder blue butterfly with splashes of purple. My transformation, although in plain sight, was largely invisible to others. Much of what I learnt back then was about how to survive as an invisible practitioner.

Wisdom I wish I had known

Throughout it all, there have been ups and downs, times of discomfort and disagreements and also many times of delight and great insight. I often reflect on the past years and what advice I might have given myself at the start of the journey. I will share with you three things I would whisper into my own ears if I knew then what I know now.

When you are new and inexperienced in a discipline you will come across people who will not listen to you because you are new and inexperienced. You might think this will disappear over time. It won't. You will hit this problem because you are young, because you are older, because you are male, because you are female, because you have not been an academic, because you are an academic, because you are a systems thinking practitioner, because you are not a systems thinking practitioner. It does not go away. You will ALWAYS come across people who will not listen to you or take you seriously. Do not waste your time making excuses for what is happening. Instead, use your energy to develop effective strategies for dealing with it. If you come across a situation where every strategy you can think of fails, move on. To some degree, you will always be invisible to someone.

As you move on from being a brand-new beginner, understand that you have moved on. You are not at the start line anymore. Continually refresh your development plans. Make sure they continue to challenge you. If they do not scare you a little, they are not ambitious enough. Develop them even when you feel invisible and in spite of being invisible. They are still valid and so are you. Do not wait for others to recognise your journey before you move on. If you do, you will never move forwards.

There will be times when your working life goes wrong. When those whom you thought you worked well with disappoint you. There will be times when trust is broken and people betray you. There will be times when you are disappointed in yourself. There will be times when you think everything is going wrong and your confidence leaves you. Add this to feeling invisible and things can feel a little grim. These times are temporary. If you hit times like these, remember why you are in this game. Never let your own purpose leave you. Always find your way back to what you love doing.

Crossing the bridge

As I have previously mentioned, crossing the bridge to me is when we make systems thinking approaches come to life in the real world. It is where we might confront challenges and barriers of using systems thinking and learn how to best deal with them. It is also where we can realise what things can present as opportunities in front of us.

It is on the bridge where we might go off down rabbit holes and into the dark, ominous forests of deep discovery. It is where we start to develop our systems thinking habits and try out our own approaches. It is where our deep inner self-development occurs, where we take time to reflect and sometimes go through the punishing lessons that teach us our craft. I think we continually cross the bridge in our practice. As soon as we arrive at the other side, feeling refreshed and confident, there is a new challenge ahead and a new bridge to cross.

As I have mentioned, the bridge can be a precarious place, with broken wooden slats, fraying rope and the threat of falling through the air into the dangerous, gushing white water below. We can get to the other side, however, and we can work to strengthen the bridge for next time. The area on the bridge is where we can feel most invisible and most vulnerable as we work on our process of deep exploration, both of the situations we are engaging with and of ourselves.

It is on the bridge where we can learn how to make systems thinking work in real life. It is where we can work out how to manoeuvre seemingly immovable obstacles and open up possibilities we would never have dreamt of. It is a place where we can build our inner confidence and get to the other side with renewed hope in what might have seemed like an impossible situation. It is where we support each other to be vulnerable and where we learn. It is our bridge of discovery, development, and hope.

Planting trees for others to sit under

Nowadays, there are many ways for practitioners to link up with and support each other whilst crossing the bridge. Far more than when I was first developing my systems practice. This does not necessarily take away our invisibility cloak though, and I find that it is deep inside ourselves that we find ways of coming to terms with being an invisible catalyst for change and improvement.

We observe, we seek to understand and we work with and within the situations we engage with day in and day out. We take actions that no one will ever know about. Make plans that no one will hear about. We manoeuvre in and around things like an invisible ghost, nudging, encouraging, guiding. We put the foundations down for what might come next. It is the solid grounding to enable the next stage of change and improvement to thrive. There is no glory. Most people do not even know what we are doing. Then, we move on, knowing that we have shuffled what needed shuffling and planted seeds that needed planting. We supported what needed supporting and sometimes, removed what needed removing. Then we walked away and started on something else. It is a huge win that feels like a failure. It feels like a failure because we have been conditioned to perceive a positive or a win as something we get immediate recognition and glory for. But a true win is when we have planted the seeds that few others even know are there, but they may benefit from in the future.

My final words of encouragement to anyone who is feeling invisible and acting as an invisible catalyst, is to look inside of yourself to feel your win, remembering to find your way back to what you love doing at the same time. The inner self is the only person who needs to know. Comfort yourself that you planted the seeds. The seeds will develop into trees that will grow and thrive for many years to come. The trees may even support other trees and encourage the growth of even newer trees. The connection between the person and the legacy is sometimes invisible to the eyes of many but it is never invisible inside of yourself.

Chapter 7: The practitioner's journey – the emotional journey

Frustration, guilt and shame

I have just come out of another one-to-one coaching session with a client. The discussion we had was along the lines of many I have had before. She started by saying, 'Now you've shown me these systems thinking approaches, I can see my organisation really differently. I can see so much stuff that I couldn't see before. Pauline, it makes me feel so frustrated that I couldn't see them before and so ashamed and guilty about that. Is this mess my fault? I should have made things work so much better.' She was a senior leader in public services who had been on her systems thinking journey for about a year.

'First of all, it's not your fault.' I was firm in my response. 'What you are dealing with is a big systemic mess. It wasn't created by one person, no one person is to blame for it, and it won't be put right by just one person either.' The pattern was a familiar one. It came along as frequently as the invisibility cloak. The same emerging feelings of frustration, guilt and shame when systems thinking opens up a whole new world right in front of your eyes for the first time. It is like pulling back a thick black curtain to reveal a multidimensional world beyond.

You do not know, however, if the people in this new colourful, intriguing, world are friend or foe. You see things you could not see before and realise the opportunities they present. This can be an exciting and invigorating time as your eyes devour the feast before them. It can also be quite a hard pill to swallow that often sticks part way down the throat, boring into your oesophagus and causing substantial discomfort. The guilt and shame can feel like a giant tidal wave looming high up in the sky has hurtled to earth at significant speed and hit you full force and knocked you flat on your back.

Remember that bridge? You are on it. You have a sense that the first wooden slat you put your foot on has crumbled and started to give way underneath you. You get a sight of the bubbling white rapids below. Then panic rises in your throat as you see nothing but frayed rope holding the next slat to the rest of the bridge.

Next, frustration builds. You feel the churning in your stomach, the tightness in your chest, your wildly beating heart and sweaty palms. First of all, it is frustration with yourself. Frustration for not seeing and for not knowing or understanding, which is irrational as we are all in an ongoing process of learning. Then comes the additional treat of the frustration you feel when others cannot see what you can now see. You have already been hit by the personal guilt and shame tidal wave. You have staggered your way out of it, feeling a little bruised and dishevelled. Now you have been unceremoniously sucked up inside a frustration tornado. It has picked you up, spun you around, turned you upside down and now it is about to fiercely expel you onto the grass below. You hit the ground with a hard, crashing bang! It can feel like it has broken every bone in your body. How do I know? Because I have been there myself. I have also heard the same story from dozens of other practitioners. It is the emotional element that can accompany a practitioner's journey. The element that is rarely shared and yet, in one-to-one discussions, I hear the same stories and feelings articulated repeatedly.

When it happened to me, I was overwhelmed. I had few support mechanisms in place, and it felt frightening, bewildering and lonely. I felt like I no longer fit in my organisation. I could not agree with many of the organisational strategies anymore and yet I still had to implement them. I knew the systemic picture was not being seen and every time I talked, I felt like I was shrivelling up as I appeared to be speaking in a language from another galaxy. I went through a whole range of emotions during this time. Am I getting it wrong? Is it me who does not understand? Why do I see things differently? I don't fit here anymore! I have no-one to talk to about this! Wow, this is a lonely place!

It was a lonely place for several years. The best way to get on in the organisation I worked for was to conform to the corporate culture and just get on with it. I was even told, at one stage to, 'not so bloody ethical!' and it would be easy for me to climb even further up the ladder. I like the person who said this to me, and I know they genuinely wanted to give me a leg up the career ladder.

I cannot tell you how hard I wished I could just go along with it . Try as hard as I might, I just could not do it. Even to this day, I wish I could have. Even to this day, I still cannot. Even in times when I sit unable to pay my rent with only singular pounds in the bank account, I cannot just go along with things I fundamentally do not agree with. So, for me, guilt, shame and frustration have been regular visitors on my journey, particularly in the early days. I tended to meet them on almost every bridge. Frustration turned out to be an unrelenting companion on the bridges I crossed. It would sit under the bridge in wait for me and pounce the minute I put my foot on the first wooden slat. Our regular tête-a-tête meetings have carefully conditioned me to deal with these emotions differently nowadays. I have developed my craft in this department over the years, but it has taken a significant personal development plan to do that.

One day

It was 2:43 pm on a warm and windy day in September 2018. The windows in the room spanned the whole of the wall and the view looked out over the beautiful rolling hills beyond. 'You don't half do some funny diagrams, Pauline. You always make me laugh.' The tone was not friendly, it was undermining. I was reminded that everyone in the room had their place and mine was clearly below the person commenting. The work we were looking at was messy, it was highly politically sensitive and as one senior leader said to me, 'It's embarrassing that we don t know why we are in the state we are in and that we don't know what to do about it . They knew me, they had worked with me before and they knew that over the coming weeks, I would open their eyes to what might well be painful, challenging and exposing. There was bound to be nervousness in the room, what else could I expect?

I was working in a business consultant capacity on a major service review in the NHS as part of a strategy development exercise. I had been brought in to, 'tell us what's going on and what we need to do . The guidance was not much more than that. It rarely was with this client. The commissioning organisation I was helping was going through major changes, and they were integrating with a local authority. Staff did not know whether they still had jobs, provider organisations in the area were crumbling under the weight of financial cuts and everyone, and I mean everyone, appeared disorientated and stressed.

The diagram, by the way, was a VSM of a service I had been reviewing. I had spent the previous few weeks out and about talking to a range of different people, looking at data and observing working practices and relationships on the ground. I had been ignored (I was obviously wearing the invisibility cloak that day), embraced, cried on, shouted at, hugged and been through a range of emotions myself from anger to frustration to empathy. The situation was not a good one. Vulnerable people were in need and the services were finding it impossible to respond. Everyone was pleading for help, blaming each other and tensions were high. Every day, I had to control my emotions and work with professionalism. Every night brought a few tears at having listened to distressing patient and family stories. A funny diagram, indeed.

'Can't you just fill in some template and write a paper and then we can tell the service they need to put it right? It's their service, they should fix it.' The template was a Word document with a single box on it. The title Service Review was lurking in the top left corner. They clearly wanted action but the responsibility for making change appeared to be like a hot potato. I guessed that they were just stuck in the moment, like a statue unable to move. It was a situation that was exacerbated by the overwhelming weight on everyone's shoulders.

Over the previous weeks I had experienced silo working, broken processes, long waiting lists, a completely broken management system, a lack of performance management, a lack of data, co-ordination mechanisms that had not worked effectively for years, a single medical consultant who was being scapegoated and a system that was broken, I mean severely broken, at three levels of recursion – the services, the individual organisations and the relationships between organisations. Inside my head, I was screaming as my little friend frustration made an appearance and seemed to be doing a taunting dance right in front of me.

On the outside, 'I'll have a chat with the clinical director, just to give her an update and then I'll come back to you', I said calmly. I decided not to argue it out but to take another approach. I needed to make the current situation clearer for them, without hurting them in the process, and that might come across better in a one-to-one meeting with the person who held some clinical responsibility. I was lucky enough to get a meeting the next day.

I did not explicitly use the VSM to explain the extent of the issues. Instead, I explained that even if the service improved to the very best of its current ability, it would not be likely to make the required difference, and I showed her how and why, using the VSM in my head to structure my narrative. I left the technical language well inside my mind. I backed myself up with evidence – a pile of failed improvement plans, the waiting lists, the cancelled appointments, the lack of staff and how far the service was from where it wanted to be. I talked about the environment and how it had changed and how the current service might soon become unfit for purpose. I explained about the lack of cross-organisational relationships at a management and service level and the inability of a large organisation, in which the service sat, to devote the attention required to move the situation to a better place. I used a range of perspectives to get the picture across from a variety of angles. I used my VSM work as a guide to build a narrative that fit together, made sense and gave a clear picture. It had become obvious that the system at a higher level of recursion was not working well and this service had become lost as a result, invisible to management, and it needed help.

The clinical director appeared relieved that we kept away from the blame game in the conversation. She never imagined that the service needed so much help. I felt a rising frustration as I was talking but I could not let it show. After all, this was a systemic issue and no one person or organisation was responsible for its current state.

The good news was that she was very responsive and there had already been some discussions about the potential for a whole new governance structure and programme of improvements. My narrative provided the evidence that would ensure it happened and it would be one of the most significant positive changes that this area of work had experienced in many years. I decided to capitalise on the value of the insights by explaining that they could be used to craft assurances to the health scrutiny committee, local councillors and patient groups. If we started to make changes, it would pacify the senior leaders in what could have been a volatile situation for them. The narrative I provided legitimised the decision-making behind the need for change. Instead of remaining in a position of weakness and despondency, the organisation and its partners had the potential to move to a position of understanding and strength. Oh, my VSM diagram? I quietly filed it under 'O' for 'one day'.

The situation was a very standard one. As I imagined, the range of emotions I experienced was wide and varied but, on this occasion, I was well prepared. Many internal colleagues and clients (if you are a consultant) cannot meet you on the same level in terms of systems thinking, as they have often not explored either themselves or the situation to the same extent you might have done when developing your practice. They do not know what they do not know and cannot see what they cannot see. Just like you did not know what you did not know in the beginning. In addition, we also know that we all have areas of unknowns, anyway. It is perfectly normal.

Effective practitioners know this about themselves and can learn to open up the exploration so that it can expose some of their unknowns as well as those of the people around them. Some people I have worked with or for, however, have never even considered that there might be things they do not know about, and this can create a build-up of frustration as you do the work. There is also the notion, of course, that they are aware of areas of unknowns for them, but they do not want anyone else to open up and expose those things. They are comfortable in their position of control and power and do not want you rocking the boat. My diagram was one such thing that was capable of rocking the boat with a certain individual, and I felt certain that they knew it. Instead of fighting that, I decided to go straight to the person with some personal responsibility in the situation to show them how I could help them. It is a strategy I have adopted over time, as I have developed my systems practice and it can often take away any feelings of uneasiness. It can, instead, come across as helping someone personally, to achieve the outcomes they are responsible for.

The emotional toll

Feelings of frustration, guilt and shame are inevitable when unearthing the less talked about aspects of a situation. Another example came from when I was working with a group of local authority staff. Some of what I experienced left me not just frustrated but deeply troubled. I came across teams who were severely broken in every way. Individuals were repeatedly on sick leave because they were ground down by the stress of trying to cope. They were surviving in an organisation which had employed several tactics to try and deal with their impossible situation. Many of the tactics did not sit well with the staff and it showed on the faces of everyone I met. At the end of the work, I took a holiday before starting something new, because of the emotion of uncovering the extent of the carnage and experiencing what they had to deal with every day.

As a practitioner, you may often unexpectedly open up wounds in a situation. Emotions around you might be running high and it is important to consider self-care as you do this. I know many a good practitioner who has turned their back on the work because it has been too troubling. The people you engage with along the way may be filled with anxiety, stress and despondency. When you work amongst it every single day, it can take its toll. In my opinion, it is exceptionally important to have strategies in place to help you deal with this element of the work. I learnt the hard way by diving in headfirst, without having strategies in place. It was painful. I suffered deeply at times, but I learnt. If you are a practitioner who has jumped in and you are currently engulfed in the emotional journey, do not despair. It gets easier as you develop your strategies for dealing with the emotions that arise as you engage in this kind of work. I would encourage you to talk to other practitioners about it. You are not alone.

Turning off the systems thinking lens

An occupational hazard of being a practitioner is that it is very difficult to turn off your skills and give yourself a break. Holidays are one of my strategies for dealing with the difficult elements of being a practitioner. They are important to maintain my wellbeing and I try to take at least two holidays a year. That said, I cannot always turn off the systems thinking lens, even when I am on holiday, and this is something I want to emphasise to other practitioners who are starting out on their journey.

I was on holiday in Northumberland, the place where I love to meander quietly along the coast in delightful solitude and take photographs. I am particularly passionate about the bird life on the Northumberland coast, especially on the Farne Islands, a place I try and visit every year. My visit was a bit of a shock though. Did I have the peaceful low-key trip to an amazing bird colony that I usually had? No, absolutely not. It was quite the opposite. There had been a run of television programmes set in Northumberland, prior to my visit. Entertaining programmes, which I particularly enjoyed. The trouble was that it brought many new people to Northumberland in their droves, eager to see the sights they had witnessed on their TV screens. 'Well, it's good for tourism,' I hear you say. But is it?

Applying system thinking to the scenario, which I automatically defaulted to doing, I considered a number of factors. The number of tourists visiting the bird colony had significantly increased. This could easily lead to a greater risk of disturbing the nesting birds. Might there be a chance that some of the birds would leave the islands as a result? I know the National Trust has good protection regulations in place to guard against this, but there were an awful lot of boat trips circling the islands. What happens next? Might people forget about the television programmes in two to five years and stop coming to the area? Might the birds have already left by then to find somewhere quieter, having been frightened off by the amount of people?

The regular nature lovers, who usually holiday in Northumberland for peace and quiet may have found somewhere else to go as well. Somewhere where they could find their usual tranquillity. The result, of course, could potentially be a short-term boom in tourism for the area but longer-term damage to tourism as people who would usually come year after year drift off elsewhere. There is also, of course, the element of cost to consider. The rise in tourists had, and continues to, push prices up. There are lots of unintended consequences that could happen in this scenario. But what is my point in considering all of this, you ask? My point is that as a practitioner, it is very hard to turn off the systems thinking lens, even when you are on holiday. This is something you, like me, might need to learn to deal with. In the meantime, I shall welcome my little friend frustration along with its teeny tiny suitcase and walking boots and hope that it remains relatively quiet.

All in all, as a practitioner, the emotional journey can be an unexpected rollercoaster. There are the general emotions of engaging with a situation to consider. There are also the emotions that arise when surviving as a practitioner in the competitive world of work. The emotions when you just cannot switch off the systems thinking lens whilst engaging with situations you care about. It is a never-ending journey and at times it can be pretty exhausting. Of course, feelings of elation are in the mix too. Not all of the emotions are negative ones. There is a feeling of delight when you make improvements and a calm and happiness as you support people to make their work lives a bit easier. There is a feeling of empathy as people tell you their stories and a sense of wonder as you explore new situations.

As a practitioner, I tend to see systems wherever I look. It can be quite scary at times. You cannot turn it off, other people around you cannot see what you can see, it brings a whole new dimension to your world, and it can be an emotional journey. Wherever you go, whatever you do, it can be like your personal angel or gremlin popping up to say hello.

Chapter 8: The practitioner's journey – forming habits

Habits, not scale

It is our habits that matter, not scale necessarily. Embodied systems thinking habits. Let's explore this further.

I was on Twitter the other day and I saw someone say that they were now not just looking at what their team did, but they needed to consider how their team worked with teams from other organisations. They termed this as going 'straight from team thinking to systems thinking.' Nice try, but just because you change the boundary of what you are doing to encompass a wider scale, it does not automatically mean you are 'systems thinking'.

It is important to understand that for a lot of practitioners, systems practice is about embodying systems thinking ideas and concepts. It is about how we go about our daily business. It is about the systems thinking habits that we form. Our systems thinking habits enable us to deeply engage with and explore the situations we encounter. I mean really see them, from several angles and perspectives and using different framings or lenses. Some of the habits we form are habits related to observation, exploration and understanding. This habitual exploration might span from a scale that is focused on our own inner psyche right up to the scale of working across large geographical areas and even beyond.

The scale does not really matter. It is the development of our systems thinking habits that matters. It is our habits that help us to observe, explore, engage and question in a systems thinking informed way. Our habits support us to discuss, debate and challenge. Our habits enable us to point out patterns of system behaviour and make visible hidden or unspoken patterns. It is about embodying habits, not just working at a different scale.

Identity and habits

As a practitioner, I have developed and will continue to develop my practice in a way that enforces the identity I assign to myself. We might be invisible, and we might have an emotional journey but generally, these are not things we aspire to. I aspire to be a meaningful and purposeful practitioner who effectively puts systems thinking into practice. To do this, I need meaningful and purposeful habits that are a representation of my embodiment of systems thinking. For me, this is what forms my identity as a systems thinking practitioner.

My identity includes having the ability to zoom in and zoom out and look at a situation from several different angles. It is the ability to consider a range of different perspectives, from the points of view of people who might have a different perspective to my own. It is the ability to recognise and overcome dogmatism and reductionism. It is the ability to recognise bias and know what part the ego is playing in a situation. It is the ability to understand what boundary judgements are being made and recognise the interconnectivity and interdependencies at play and their implications. It is re-framing situations to open up new opportunities. It is using appropriate system theories to inform my practice. It is self-reflecting and learning. It is about so many more habits than this. It is all about systems thinking habits, formed over years.

Systems thinking habits form part of my behaviour which feeds into my self-assigned identity. The prouder I become about forming systems thinking habits, the stronger I feel my identity is as a practitioner and the harder I aim to develop my skills.

This feedback loop of linking habits to behaviours and aligning them with identity, in turn, feeding the desire to develop habits has become a key element of my practice and work. I have seen how the notion of identity can make or break a person. I am thinking back to the social workers I was engaging with several years ago. One thing that was severely distressing to them was that they felt that their identity was becoming confused. That they were not able to enact the habits they recognised as good social work practice. This was because they were being forced to cut back their support to people. Their identity was no longer the caring social worker who gave people the support they needed. Their identity was about how they coped with severely lower levels of funding, which meant not giving people the support they needed. The impact on their identity was absolutely huge as the habits they were forced to adopt started to become their persona. As a practitioner, it is about the habits you form, not the scale at which you are working, necessarily.

Growing

One thing I would urge practitioners to consider is reviewing and upgrading their habits as they grow. It can be all too easy to get stuck in the same habits when the rest of the world has moved on. I have learnt that reviewing my habits regularly, upgrading them and working to embed newer, fresher habits is a way of continually upgrading my identity as a practitioner. It is not an easy thing to do though, and I cannot say it comes easily to me. Even just today, as I am writing this, someone reminded me that I had fallen into a thinking trap that was putting a particular slant on a situation I faced. He reminded me to let my reframing habit kick in. I did. It opened up a whole new way forward for me. It took maybe two minutes to unveil several new ways forward in a situation I had perceived as being stuck. Having someone to remind you every now and then can be a very effective prompt.

No more heroes

Be radical! Just do it! Ninja. Guru. Thought leader. Evolutionary. Superpower. These and other such phrases are words I see quite a lot in the world of systems thinking. Reading them brings about images of potentially large-scale, radical change, developed and implemented by people with some kind of excess of creative and intellectual capability. I also see words such as revolutionary, new and rebel, as if we have to do something that is completely different to anything that has ever been tried before.

I am now going to suggest that these words are rarely the words used by the people I see making the most powerful and effective changes and improvements in their work situations using systems thinking. They do not wear black satin costume masks across their eyes. The only cape they wear is an invisibility cape. They barely consider themselves worthy of being listened to, never mind labelling themselves as a guru and they certainly do not have superpowers. They are people. Ordinary people, just like you and me. People with consistently good systems thinking habits.

In many of the pieces of work I have undertaken with others, it has been small-scale, frequent, persistent and repeated habits and actions that have brought about change, some of which none of us could have ever aspired to. Of course, some things were new, fresh, different and not tried before. However, it was the embodied systems thinking habits that came through in people's work that created the right conditions for the identified changes to be implemented and embedded.

For example, when we reduced hospital discharge delays to below the regional and national average by not much more than understanding perspectives and how information was communicated, building relationships, making meaning together and engaging in mutually reciprocal arrangements. None of it was a big-bang. None of us were superheroes. Heck, we were the ones hiding in locked offices, crying. But, by peer-to-peer supporting one another and engaging in systems thinking habits and using insights to implement a series of incremental changes, we made a difference together. As the enactment of systems thinking habits infected others, they changed the identity of the situation we were engaging with. Teams stopped being the discharge team from X area . They became, our colleagues on the other site. The processes in the situation changed from, 'that awful process that X hospital has in place' to, the process that we designed together that is giving me different options to deal with this current problematic situation. It was habits, not some superhero that made the difference.

Incremental vs. big bang

When working on place-based systems change, the work was not about going in and making a big bang change. It was about modelling systems thinking habits to create the right conditions with the groups I was working with so that they had an example of how to embody the habits and enact them. Once the habits were embedding, I just needed to get out of their way and let them get on with the changes and improvements they had already identified and were sitting in the back of their minds. Our sessions together changed the identity of our interactions from a workshop where someone tells us about systems change to a safe space where we can be ourselves, be vulnerable, talk about our challenges, learn new things, help each other and showcase our gifts.

It was an incremental embodiment of systems thinking habits over a period of time, rather than a big-bang. It gave the groups the space to develop their confidence to do things they had never done before, challenge things they had never challenged before and think differently about their input regarding systems change. The habits shifted theirs and the group s identity. In turn, the identity reinforced the habits and the people involved were then very well equipped and had a supportive network to make the changes they aspired to.

My message here is that it does not matter if you do not want to make a big change. Some people do and that is ok. But it is not the only way. The thought of big bang change can be excluding and in some cases repellent. It can alienate people who have great ideas. It can end up feeding the ego, rather than nurturing the soul.

Quietly embedding systems thinking habits into your practice can carry you to a place of greater enlightenment in your work. You might not hear the ringing bells and screeching whistles that those noisily flying their own flags exhibit. What is important is that you are going in the right direction, even when it does not feel like you are. It only does not feel like you are because you are conditioned to expect an immediate reward for any effective actions you take. When you are embedding your habits to strengthen your practice, it is sometimes only you who will recognise the incremental effort and improvement. The positive outcome at a wider scale might come further down the line. Do not be put off by your lack of immediate reward.

A different kind of reward

As a practitioner, we often do not get an immediate feel good-effect from our work. We challenge thinking, suggest different framings, bring different perspectives into play, etc. These things generally do not give us an immediate reward. More often than not, what we get is pushback. However, when we practise, we are often planting seeds and putting down foundations for what might come further down the line. Naturally, there might be a long delay before we see tangible results, particularly if we are working on systems change. The feedback loop has such a delay that it is easy to stop recognising it as a feedback loop. Then, because we do not immediately see the benefit of our work, it is easy for us to stop engaging in systems thinking habits, believing we have failed. I hear in conversations that this is why many practitioners find it so hard to keep going and tend to give up. There is nothing immediately telling them that their actions are effective.

Personally, I have realised that I need to understand my wins and rewards differently. I have to remind myself to continue practising my systems thinking habits, and in some cases, it has taken me years to embed a particular habit. It took me eighteen months to embed the habit of questioning how information was being exchanged and how channels of communication were or were not working. It was hard work and I have to keep practising it, in case it fades. It took me about a year to embed the habit of questioning what hidden patterns of system behaviour might be at play in a situation.

I can tell you that being a practitioner is not for the faint-hearted. There is a lot to consider and some habits may never embed. I am aware of this and regularly reflect on and review what I am doing or not doing to see if I am wandering off into the deep, dark woods totally unaware that I am there.

This is perfectly normal and part of the journey that many of us are on, even if we do not always fully understand it at the time. Frequently and consciously telling ourselves that our habits and actions are worthwhile is another element of the work that can be exhausting. It can take a lot of stamina to keep going.

Extending a hand to others

Bear in mind that every person you convince to engage with learning about systems thinking might also go through this element of the journey. It will be equally as hard for them to take the leap of faith as it was for you. It will be equally as hard for them to believe in the habits you are advocating for. It will be equally as hard for them to come to terms with the fact that there might be no element of reward in the mix for them. It will be equally as hard for them to step onto the swaying bridge of exploration and deep learning. My word of caution is to encourage others with respect for where they are in their own life journey.

The very last thing you want to do is to put someone in a position that could potentially harm them, mentally. I give this caution with a very serious tone. I have seen this happen a number of times and the outcome is not pretty. When you encourage others, make sure you are on the other side of that bridge, holding out your hand to them, just in case they feel they need to take it. The practitioner's journey can be a tough and bewildering one and I have seen it take people by surprise many times. The impact is often the same – the emergence of guilt, shame and frustration as they face the tidal wave and the tornado that they did not even see coming. You should expect that the tidal wave and tornado might be headed their way and prepare them and you for it with empathy and wisdom.

Reframing rewards

With all of this in mind, you might wonder why I am still on this journey. My personal experience is that being able to engage with a situation in a way that makes me understand it is a genuine relief – the relief is my reward. Always having at my disposal a wide range of approaches and concepts to help me understand the context of the situation takes away my fear - the reduction of my fear is my reward. When systems thinking helps me to know what actions I should not be taking – supporting me to not make a blundering mistake is my reward. Understanding the systemic nature of a situation and knowing and acknowledging that things are not my fault – that removal of guilt is my reward. It makes complex situations feel bearable. As such, it takes my stress away – this is definitely a reward.

It gives me a way to articulate what is happening in a situation – that is my reward. It enables me to lay foundations knowing that someone, somewhere, at some point in time, will not have to go through as much anguish because those foundations were laid – the feeling of having done something useful for someone else is my reward. Watching the stress melt away from the face of the client when they realise they are not to blame for a long-term systemic mess – this is my reward. Being told that articulating why things are as they are was a cathartic experience – that is my reward. Seeing the results of engaging systems thinking habits and infecting others with the enthusiasm to do the same – that is my reward. Being told that systems practice has changed someone else's life, as I have heard several times – this is a huge and overwhelming reward. There are many reasons to continue. We sometimes just have to re-frame what we classify as rewards. Once we do this, it can help us to keep going.

Chapter 9 – The practitioner's journey – ethical systems practice

Ethical systems practice

This chapter is intentionally short. This is because we could talk forever about what ethical systems practice might be and, of course, that definition will be different for each of us, depending on our perspective. It is not my intention to have that debate here but to raise some key points for consideration about ethical systems practice, from my perspective. Being ethical may not always be easy. There will be times when we might not even realise we are not being ethical. Here are points to consider.

Power, position and privilege

How might practitioners genuinely endorse systems thinking if we are misusing our own power, position and privilege? That is not systems thinking. It is dominance. How can we appropriately step away from this dominance and still thrive in our workplaces, which may have harmful power structures and people who enjoy their position and privilege? How do we check that we are not the ones abusing our power to maintain our position and control others? Genuinely doing this can be extremely difficult because, to some extent, we may have become blind to our own power, position and privilege. I see lots of claims of people devolving power but much less evidence of it actually happening. For example, the people who want to 'do' systems thinking but only if they are the ones at the forefront of using it in their workplace or if they are in charge of any systems thinking projects or they are the ones dominating what is classed as systems thinking and what is not.

Diverse perspectives

How might practitioners genuinely put systems thinking into practice if we refuse to take diverse perspectives into consideration? How do we go about bringing diverse perspectives into our work? Are there times when it may not be appropriate to do so? All too often I see the perspectives of one similar group of people being considered and those perspectives are expected to represent a much wider diversity of people. How do we engage in systems thinking if we only ever converse with or listen to people who look and sound like us?

Congruence

How might practitioners endorse an approach that relies heavily on relationships if we are complacent and refuse to validate the knowledge, ingenuity and gifts of others? All others. Even those we do not agree with. How might we endorse an approach that advocates for boundary critique if we refuse to recognise and appreciate the perspectives of others? How might we advocate for trust and sharing, if we are willing to cheat, lie and take actions that are to the detriment of others? How might we advocate for effective communication if we are dogmatic dictators ourselves? Do you think we recognise when we are? How might we effectively consider purpose if we project our own purposes onto others and refuse to acknowledge the purposes they ascribe to themselves? How can we genuinely claim to be the bearer of an approach that will liberate people, whilst we might be (sometimes unknowingly) oppressing others?

We are human too and we can easily fall into these traps. How might we develop ways of enabling reflective conversations if we are not willing to self-reflect and include ourselves and our own behaviours as part of that process? How do we advocate for reciprocation if we take from others but never give back?

How do we be participative if we are the ones who actively push others out of the group so that we can be the big fish in the pond? How do we consider feelings, whilst actively seeking to destroy others for our own gain? How do we claim humility when

172

we might spend our time combatively positioning ourselves against others and boasting about our claims? Competition can be healthy but combat in systems thinking often is not. How can we claim to believe in human flourishing if our actions are weighted towards only ourselves flourishing, without much thought for others? How do we work with empathy if we do not have empathy for those who are jealous of us? Are systems thinking practitioners wise? How can we be wise if we cannot see the irony that sits all around us, making spectacular claims whilst demonstrating none of them?

Practising ethically is not just a phrase to bandy around in a glossy magazine, written by a business consultant, to make us look good. The more genuine way is to demonstrate ethical practice in our habits. Our brains need to adapt to new habits, however, bearing in mind that we may not even know of our bad habits. Our current habits may have become so ingrained that we are blind to them. We might accept them as the norm and assume everyone else is the same.

Of course, there are likely to be many practitioners out there who do not care deeply about the discipline and may not be too concerned about practising ethically. Their practice may be more superficial. They may not acknowledge the needs, preferences, issues and concerns of others. We are all free to practice as we see fit. We can, however, get a rather large negative kickback when this happens and here is the reason why. If practitioners are more superficial in their approach and do not really want to apply the thinking as deeply as they can, they may not understand or engage with the depth of nuance that brings about the power of systems thinking. It may be invisible to them. In some cases, this might well be an effective strategy for those who do not want or need to venture very deeply into systems thinking.

It can, however, be a constraint to other practitioners when this is the approach taken by someone dominating the field. Why? Because they may not be exposing others to the full benefits of systems thinking. As result, I have experienced people thinking that there is no substance to systems thinking and they give up on it, believing that it is nothing but the next fad. This is a phenomenon I have witnessed many times. In recent years, I have seen it become more prevalent in my working arenas. Some people I have talked to say that they have already given up on systems thinking because they think it does nothing for them. It makes me quite sad because I always feel like they have never given it a real chance.

As systems thinking has become more popular, what I see happening quite often is people jumping on the systems thinking bandwagon, so that they can prove their worth and hold onto either their jobs or their clients. They cling to consultancy models like they are pots of gold which are going to save the day. They won't. The depth of the original thinker and creator can easily become lost. The ideas are then in danger of being followed by the masses in a superficial way.

Very little truly comes quickly. It takes time and effort, and it is very often an uncomfortable journey. If your journey has been anything less, you may want to ask yourself how it got to such a point so quickly. I know I have worked on my own personal systems thinking approach for over sixteen years and I am just scratching the surface and have such a lot still to learn. In reality, many people carry on working in exactly the same way as they always have. They just project new words over the top of the same old things they have always done. In my opinion, this is why systems thinking can be more powerful when it is separated from academic prestige and money-making to become a series of habits for all to apply over time.

Rectitude

I recently came across the word, 'rectitude' in a book by Joe Navarro, a former FBI agent. In his book *Be Exceptional,* he explains that rectitude is about moral, upright, ethical and honourable behaviour (Navarro, 2021). I think this is a great description of what an ethical systems thinking practitioner could be. Setting an example for no other reason than because you can. Over the years, I have learnt that some of the most effective practitioners are very moral. They are humble and ethical and honourable.

Yet we have an issue here, don't we? Being humble is not generally a trait that organisations tend to look for in their senior managers. Sadly, it does not seem to be a good selling point for practitioners in goal-seeking organisations. With a lack of encouragement or support, being a humble practitioner can make you feel very vulnerable. It requires courage. Courage to maintain your boundaries. Courage not to follow the crowds just to make life easier and courage to keep going when you are invisible.

No one can dictate a one and only way to be an ethical systems thinking practitioner. It is for you to decide your own identity and how you like to work and for what purpose. Most practitioners have a unique style that emerges over time. One thing I would say, though, is to consider the impact on everyone else if you choose not to be an ethical practitioner. Are you helping or hindering? Collaborating or competing? Supporting or disabling? Creating or destroying? Being a practitioner is one thing. How you be a practitioner is another.

Speaking out

Some practitioners say that it is our ethical duty to speak out when it matters. It is for the good advancement of our discipline. I would say that how you speak out is important. If the way you speak out destroys others, it is not really likely to be effective at engaging others to learn about systems thinking.

I also feel that you need to be aware of the risks when you speak out. Speaking truth to power is fine, as long as you are aware of and accept the potential risks when you do so.

Chapter 10 – The practitioner's journey - internal agent or business consultant?

If you are embarking on your systems thinking journey, you may be weighing up whether it is better to work as an internal agent, employed by an organisation or an external consultant. I reflect on my experiences of both, to help you make the right decision for you at this point. But first, a short story to get the discussion started.

The boys club

Back in the 1970s my friend Pamela and I defiantly stood on the steps of the local Boys Club, keen to find a way in. Week after week, we turned up. We watched the young boys playing pool and badminton through the windows and we were turned away. We protested and were turned away. We turned up again and sat in the doorway, blocking everyone s way, in silent protest. We were turned away. We came back again and again and again, week after week until the person manning the doors changed. Gone was the battle axe of a woman (who was one of our teachers) with her booming voice and obvious dislike of children.

In came a younger male youth worker. He came out and talked to us, and asked us why we, two young girls, kept coming back and trying to join the Boys Club. Well, there are no clubs for girls, and we aren't into baking, sewing and skipping anyway. We want to do sport and play pool and badminton. We can pay our entry fee and we think it is unfair that we aren't allowed in when there is nothing else for us to do in the area . We put forward a rational and well thought-through argument. After all, we had plenty of time to think about it sat on their doorstep week after week. He let us in.

The battle axe came back and asked why we were inside. After some heated discussion between them, she left, angry and red-faced. We never knew what was said, but we became members of the Boys Club and so did some of our other girlfriends. In fact, that male youth worker worked one-on-one with a very close friend of mine, usually in the middle of the badminton hall as she was hitting shuttlecocks, to help her overcome her stutter. No one had ever done that for her before and we were all elated when she showed off her newfound confidence in getting through a sentence without one stutter at all. We even got our faces on the front page of the local newspaper for doing work with the wildlife warden from the local dene. We helped to clear shrubbery so that a pathway in the woods could be created. It was the very first pathway in what is now a thriving woodland, visited by many people every day, walking for leisure and exercising their dogs. We gave back to our community for our time in the Boys Club. I bet the battle axe's face was a picture when she picked up her paper in the morning and we were right on the front page with Mr. Monk, the wildlife warden, representing the Boys Club.

The moral of this story is not the male/ female argument, although it clearly could be about that. It is about the concept of who is in and who is out, what that feels like and what the implications of that might be. When it comes to being a practitioner working in a position in an organisation that is not high up in the hierarchy, you can easily feel out of the gang. Senior managers may not identify you as someone who has something useful to say. If you are an external business consultant, you can easily feel out of the gang. You do not really know the nuance in a situation and the staff think that you are just there to take their ideas and make money out of them.

Both positions can be demoralising and demotivating when you know others might benefit from hearing your ideas. Both internal agents and consultants can feel like they are out of the gang at times. I have worked as both, so here are my reflections, in hope that they are useful if you are making a decision about whether to work as an internal agent or a consultant.

The internal agent

The argument I hear most often from practitioners working inside an organisation as a member of staff is that people at a more senior level do not take them seriously. I hear you. I really do. I have been in that position also, frequently. You are stuck in a hierarchy and the person above you has never contemplated that you might have more knowledge and expertise than they have about anything because they are higher up the hierarchy and therefore believe they know more than you about absolutely everything. They have never contemplated the fact that you might have met yourself at a deeper level than they will ever meet themselves. They deem it their absolute duty to keep you in your box and never use the skills and talents you have. I mean, they would not want you looking better than them, would they? There is too much at stake. Your presence as a thinking feeling human being with a wealth of gifts can often be well and truly under that invisibility cloak.

It can be even worse if you do not have the persona of a loud, confident person running around at one thousand miles per hour to get things done, at pace . I hate that phrase. Isn't it awful? It is my experience that more often than not, confidence, being loud and being seen are perceived as being much better than having skills, knowledge and insight. I will not pretend this does not happen, because I know it does.

There are, however, organisations where people have lots of autonomy, are respected and listened to and when this is the case, your systems practice can be on fire. I was lucky enough to spend several years in such a position as a commissioner in the NHS. I worked for a director who sat me down and showed me his objectives. He made clear the boundaries of what would get me, him and the organisation into trouble. He told me how he liked his decisions to be made. He told me which governance processes needed adhering to. He talked to me about when to ask him something and when to just get on with it .

I knew my boundaries and I knew his expectations. I was told to, 'Do what you need to do, just don't get us into bloody trouble!' I loved his style. It was direct, clear and no messing around. 'I'll always have your back. Even if you do something wrong. I might go mad about it behind the scenes, but I will always have your back. I don't have time for messing around.' His trust in me to do the right thing was an essential starting point. I worked my back off for our organisation because of the feeling of being trusted to do what needed to be done. I went above and beyond whenever it was necessary, and I always felt supported. I did some excellent systems thinking work in that role and we all benefitted.

Then, one day I heard, 'Pauline what the bloody hell have you been doing? The Strategic Health Authority is coming here tomorrow to see me about your area of work!' I shrugged. They came. They met with my director to praise him for all of the hard work he had done as the results were clearly showing. Do you know what he said when they left? I was not there but I was reliably informed that he stood up in the senior managers' office and shouted, 'We're all messing around focusing on X and Pauline s out there saving our bloody arses and none of us even knew about it.'

Most people in the office had a great relationship with him. He was excellent to work for and I totally appreciate the time we had together. It was definitely a contributor to the kind of practitioner I am today. I learnt the value of trust. You know, I could even go into a meeting with him with external stakeholders where I had no time to brief him about our direction of travel before the meeting. I could write on a piece of paper, 'Don't let them do X. Make sure they do Y. Do not let them out of the room unless they agree to do it.'

That is all I would give him, and he would argue it with 100% commitment. We would get the result we needed, virtually every time. I trusted him to go with my suggestion. He trusted that I would make the right decision and not make a fool of him, and I would not cross the boundaries that had been set. I have a lot of fondness for the time in which I learnt those lessons. I learnt about the power of explicitly defining boundaries. I learnt about openness and honesty. I learnt how to make decisions. I learnt how to trust myself. I learnt about the right balance of autonomy. I learnt about treating each other as human beings and looking out for one another.

The working relationship was a very relaxed human one and yet we were dealing with some exceptional challenges, which were often highly political in nature.

That was not the only time I have been supported to work with autonomy and showcase my skills. I worked for several other managers who are now my friends. One of which I have talked about already in this book. From her, I learnt what it meant when a manager feels happy and fulfilled in their own lives. How it can impact you as they do not fall into the traps of jealousy and game playing. That manager encouraged me to use my systems thinking skills to the full and even started to learn some of the skills herself. She was curious and very appreciative of the skills I brought to her team. She advocated for my work frequently and encouraged others to have sessions with me so that I could share my approaches. She was more than a manager. She was a friend. She supported me personally and I felt totally loyal to her in return. I was sad when I chose to move on from her team. I wanted to spread my systems thinking wings further and I always knew that with change and moving forward, often comes loss. Not seeing each other every day and being part of our lovely team was a loss. What I gained as an internal agent was a feeling of being in by being part of something bigger that felt special.

But what do you do if you are a practitioner who is an internal agent and you are not being seen? Not being included or listened to? You are not 'in'. One thing I have done in times like this is to continue to do what I can within the span of my autonomy. I have learned to take a show, don't tell approach. There is no point complaining about your assumed lack of worth. It just makes you feel really bad, reinforcing the negative feelings and spiralling you down into a pit of demotivation. Make opportunities for yourself, even if they are small ones. When you do this, you are developing your practice, regardless. You are building your skills, regardless. You are developing your portfolio, regardless. Whilst it may not feel like it, you are moving forwards. What is the alternative? Do none of this?

There is always a way to get something out of the situation, even if it is not everything you would like to happen. The manager who likes to keep you quiet cannot stop you from developing yourself and making the best of the opportunities which are there. There is always an opportunity to learn and develop. Granted, it may not be what you aspire to, but it can help to think to yourself, 'Which part of me can I develop here?' and concentrate on that, rather than your oppressive, often micro-managing manager who feels the need to control you. Do not give them space in your head. They do not deserve it.

Over time, if you continue to make effective change, you never know who might spot it. I had no idea the Strategic Health Authority had eyes on the outcomes of the work I was doing. My learning from that is that someone, somewhere, is always watching, whether you know it or not.

The external business consultant

Being an external business consultant has felt completely different for me. I have long-term clients who I work very well with and I have built up some strong relationships with the staff I have met. The human element can still be enacted as an external business consultant. There are, however, downsides.

As an external consultant, I find it far more difficult to engage with the nuance in a situation. Part of that is because I like to feel the energy around me. It does not take much interaction for me to pick up on whether people are scared or excited about the work. I can spot those who have reservations by watching their body language and by listening to the tone of their voice. I like to observe the interactions between the people in teams and the interactions between people and their managers. It is not hard to spot the tensions, the energy slumps or the areas of high positive energy.

Yes, I can do this as an external consultant, but it is far more difficult than when I am an internal agent. The minute a consultant is in the room, you change the situation. People can feel like they are being watched and act differently from usual. To deal with this, I spend time getting to know people and how their job feels for them. I walk past the managers to the people on the front line to find out what is really going on. It is usually only when I can show that I can see the world through their eyes and empathise with their position that I gain their trust.

Much of this is embedded in everyday working as an internal agent. These are the advantages you have. Sometimes, being less seen is a huge advantage as you can observe the dynamics in the situation without disturbing them as much. It helps you to get a more realistic view of what is going on. This is a huge advantage that internal agents often overlook because they are too busy focusing on the oppression from their managers. As a consultant, I find that I have to make purposeful and sometimes intense efforts at this stage of my explorations. As an internal agent, it comes almost without any effort at all.

One thing people say to me is that as a consultant, I will be listened to because I have been brought in to be listened to. This has some element of truth, but it is also untrue at the same time. Yes, I am listened to, but as an internal agent, there have been far more ways at my disposal to be listened to. As a consultant I rarely get the option to do the show, don't tell work, and yet I feel that this is how systems thinking is best showcased. Talking to managers about systems thinking is often pointless. They have no mental models of it, so they cannot visualise it. I tend not to talk about systems thinking, but to talk only about benefits and yet, to me, this feels quite sales-like.

Then, there are the times that I work with multiple organisations and cross boundaries with a range of people. Whilst these have been positive experiences, there have been times when I have felt my craft has been no more respected than a half-eaten Jaffa Cake. People just want to grab your materials and use them as their own. They reach out in desperation for tools because they do not want to engage in systems thinking for themselves. One day, they will realise that what they are doing is not really giving the results they aspired to. No doubt they will say that they tried that systems thinking thing and it did not help.

So, what is best? Internal agent or business consultant?

I want to throw out a challenge to anyone who manages staff in an organisation. Why should a business consultant be better than your own staff? If you think your own staff do not have the skills, why not? You are the one responsible for their training and development? Have you let them down? Do you blame your staff because you have not been able to achieve something? Are you defaulting to using business consultants because 'your issue must be a really big one?' Have you used the need to bring business consultants in to validate the fact that you have not been able to make an improvement? Do you brush aside any fairly simple suggestions for improvement because you believe your situation is unique and a simple change cannot possibly make a difference? I can tell you that very often, a small or simple change, if it is appropriately and well executed, has the potential to make a huge difference.

If you think your own staff do not have insights, why not? Have you kept them in the dark about how the organisation operates? Have you even spoken to them? Or is your mindset such that you believe that people at the lower end of the hierarchy cannot possibly have anything to teach you? Are you responsible for putting your staff in a hierarchical box and leaving them to shout into a void? Are you allowing one member of staff to dominate so that others are unable to contribute ideas? Why? Isn't engaging with lots of diverse perspectives more likely to bear fruits?

Are your staff so burnt out and demoralised that they feel unable to contribute ideas for improvement? Why? Have you not put in place ways of working that enable their wellbeing? Have you not ensured effective coordination mechanisms to absorb the complexity of the situation, so they do not absorb it personally? Have you put unrealistic expectations on your staff, meaning your expectations have not been met? Do you now blame your staff and think they have nothing useful to contribute? It hurts, doesn't it? To contemplate this if you are a manager? But it hurts no less than not being listened to.

Even if you have been this person, it is ok. No, really, it is. It can be easy to default to being this person. You are under pressure too, right? You are dealing with a big systemic mess too, right? You are struggling too, right? I see you. If you are in this category, please do not beat yourself up about it. Life is life and we cannot be perfect for the whole of our journey. There is, however, a potentially better way forward and I am sure that by now, you are starting to grasp what that is.

I would also say to the staff who feel not listened to - if your manager starts to give you opportunities and suddenly starts to believe in you and support you, if they try and make amends, let them. Stubbornly turning away and not giving them a chance does nothing but model the behaviour you do not want. Everyone has to start somewhere. Understanding that we all get it wrong sometimes is a great place to start. Managers are people too. Despite what you may think, they have feelings too. We can all be a pain in the neck sometimes and opting for curiosity and kindness is likely to get you much further in the long run.

Your internal agents have a wealth of understanding of the nuance of the situations you are trying to improve. They are often likely to come to a reasonable improvement idea much quicker than most external consultants. They are also likely to already have relationships in place that will support putting the ideas into action. They will have influence that can be effectively and rapidly used. They will understand the governance processes. You just need to believe in them. If they are not trained in approaches that can help them to help you, that is an area of sound investment. You are likely to get a much better return on your money. What I believe is a much better way forward is upskilling people in the organisation and giving them coaching to support them in the early days of applying their newfound skills.

My personal preference

My personal preference in the past has been to just get on with it as an internal agent and showcase the results. Then I told people how I did things when asked. I found that this way sparks curiosity and can yield excellent results. I do, however, like the freedom that consultancy gives me in the way I live my life. I find a nine-to-five commitment such a bind and I often struggle to fit into organisations. I tend to do a small amount of internal agent work and the rest consultancy, training and coaching. This enables me to have the security of some consistent money every month and also allows me to exercise creativity in the way I spend my time.

My advice to you would be to stop aspiring to be liked, wanted and listened to by managers who do not care about you. Just take the opportunities that you do have whilst looking for others. You do not need to be a business consultant. The grass is very often not greener. You are just imagining that it is.

Pauline Roberts

Part 4: Moving Forward

Pauline Roberts

Chapter 11: The present day

All we cannot see

In my current work, you cannot see my world. It is invisible, you see. It sits within the nuance of my own inner thinking and creating. It comes from the depths of my epistemology. My work life. My home life. My wider family life. It comes from the good times and the bad. It comes from my creative moments and my times of despair. It comes from years of working. Years of training. It comes from deep personal work, pushing through times of love and grief. There is nothing that you have experienced like I have. So, you cannot see what I see, as you are not me.

You cannot see my world. It is invisible, you see. You do not know my purpose, my inner desires and what drives me. You do not know what I came through that made me who I am. Your perspective does not come from the same place as mine. Your motivations are different from mine. You have no idea what my motivations are or what they might be in the future. You cannot see what I see, as you are not me.

You cannot see my world. It is invisible, you see. It is in every pore, every thought, every emotion and everything I do. It plays to my life desires and pushes me beyond the boundaries of my own imagination. It comes from deep within, from bright gold glittering explosions of contentment and hope from deep within my soul, but you cannot see what I see, as you are not me.

I cannot see what you see, as I am not you. Your world is as invisible as mine. I do not know what motivates you, what scares you. What drives you, what stops you in your tracks. I do not know where your perspectives come from or what shapes your behaviours. I do not know your life desires or your accomplishments to date. I do not know what you want to achieve next so I cannot seek to work towards it. I cannot see what you see, as I am not you.

So, how do I support you when you want to learn and grow if you cannot see what I see and I cannot see what you can see? Well, it is gently as we go. One step at a time. One lens at a time. One perspective at a time. One re-framing at a time. We cannot jump into a huge approach without the 'gently as we go' guiding us both through framing, using different lenses, challenging boundaries and more often than not, challenging ourselves.

'Why did I not see that straight away?' you ask. Because you were not sensitised to it and it is gently as we go. 'But why gently as we go?' you ask. Because to turn your world upside down by shaking your perspective, your perception, your framing, and the lens you use to see the world all at the same time would leave you with a deep sense of confusion, disorientation, loss, and possibly shame and guilt. My job is to guide you, not destroy you. Serve you, not harm you. Support you, not throw you over a cliff. So, particularly when I am coaching or guiding you in applying systems thinking, it is gently as we go.

This is not what most people want, though, so finding a way forward for my work can be tough. People generally want 'things' they can 'apply' to get an instant result. A slot machine that will spit out their winnings if they insert enough coins. They want a quick answer to their woes and an even quicker outcome from their efforts. They want to be in the gang and to be seen as being at the front of the race. They want to say they have done something that differentiates them from others. The ego drives them harder and harder, deeper and deeper down the wrong deep dark hole. There are plenty of people who will give them this, and even more so now than at any other time in my years as a practitioner. In the quest for quick answers and possibly to undermine anything that cannot produce them, I was asked this question recently: Is systems thinking a bit shallow, obvious and academic with no practical guidance?' It was certainly something to be contemplated, as I considered the next steps of my journey.

Shallow, obvious and academic?

At first, it would be easy for a practitioner to be a bit taken aback by this statement, offended even, especially if your practice is deeply embodied. But think about it, is the systems thinking on which we base our practice a bit obvious? Is it academic? I would have to say that my answer to this, at this point in time, is yes and no. Shallow? Well, I think that has a different answer, which I think is no. Here are my reasons.

In the UK, we live in a country where lies from our government seem to be an everyday occurrence, racism is coming out to play and underdogs are seen as merely that. We are in a global arena where the 1% rule (allegedly and it certainly feels like that is the case) and others suffer from their greed, dominance and desire to control. Systems thinking, with its relationships, reciprocation, self-organisation, emergence and feedback may seem almost like an alien concept to some. But it isn't is it? It is natural and obvious. It has been around throughout the ages, and it is in the very essence of life. We can see it all around us in nature. So, why might it seem academic, with no practical guidance?

Well, think of it like this - does your company have policies of reciprocation, with those you might traditionally see as competitors, which put the greater good of the wider system first and the selfish needs of the organisations second? In most cases, I doubt it. Do you have internal organisational protocols that reward cross-organisational collaboration and sharing? In most cases, I doubt it. Do you monitor your organisation by considering the effectiveness of its systemic sensibilities and its ability to adapt to a changing environment? In most cases, I doubt it.

Mind-numbing key performance indicators that drive perverse behaviours are far more attractive. They can be manipulated to read however you want your organisation to appear. Individuals can celebrate and gain promotion and the company can go to the top of the ratings chart. Hurrah! Do you allow teams the maximum feasible amount of autonomy, give them the authority to act and decide with them how you like decisions to be made and then let them work using their own initiative and creativity? In most cases, I doubt it.

Do you allocate resources to your departments with the intention of allowing people to make enough money to live on whilst also having a good work/ life balance? Or do you squeeze every drop of work out of them that you can, pay them as little as you can get away with and get rid of them at a drop of a hat when you want to make savings?

Would you go to your board meeting and tell your partners that you want to create the conditions for change with others, rather than compete and be the best? You would be laughed out of the boardroom in a lot of cases. It is not that there is no practical guidance. It is not that the concepts are inaccessible. It is that the practical guidance is not palatable and not in sync with our competitive, combative ways of doing business.

Our Western world has moulded us in such a way that what has become obvious to many is not collaboration but competition, not sharing but hoarding, not reciprocation but taking everything we can for ourselves. We are educated in ways that make us consider things as independent subjects. Our politics teaches us that charlatan-like behaviour wins. Many know this way is wrong and seek better ways. Through them, there is lots of practical guidance, but it is not what everyone wants to hear. This is even evident in the systems thinking community. There are often claims of collaboration and sharing and yet the reality often boils down to competition, building gangs and a need for control. To be seen as first, or more importantly, not to be seen as last.

But is systems thinking all that ? Is it the thing that will save us, make our world better and end misery on our planet? Make our organisations thrive and grow? Who knows if it can prevail over the dominant competitive control mindset? Our democracy is for sale and our internal worlds are all individually constructed by algorithms and behaviour shifting manipulation. We cannot even align our realities easily. What I see and experience every day is completely different to what my neighbour sees and experiences every day. Can systems thinking prevail in this world? Some say it can.

Personally, I think all we can do is keep trying and it starts with us. Within us. Deep inside of us. It will take for us to want to do the deep work on ourselves and I am not sure everyone wants to do this. When organisations say they want change, how many times do you think the chief executive and senior team accept that part of the change is for them to take a long hard look in the mirror at themselves? How often do you think middle managers think that they need to work on themselves? How many times might other members of staff think that they need to work on themselves? People can default to thinking that every other party apart from themselves needs to change. How many times have you heard the cry, 'We need culture change' when what people really means is, 'It's them. They aren't doing what we want them to do'. It is nothing but a blame game that sees organisations go round and round in circles like a bored dog chasing its tail. It keeps people distracted, I suppose.

So, is it obvious? It should be, but I believe our natural systems thinking capabilities have been lost somewhere along the way. We have had them almost beaten out of us, like dust out of an old rug. It is too easy for us to be goal orientated and want outcomes. We like to gain top marks, be recognised and think that we are better than others. We are a product of the world into which we were born, unfortunately. It takes for us to consciously work around such challenges to enable systems thinking to be obvious to us once again.

Is it too academic? Only if you are looking in the wrong places for inspiration and practical examples of implementation. There are lots out there. If you cannot see them, you are not looking in the right places. I also know there are a plethora of excellent practitioners doing great things, however, who will never showcase their work. Why? I asked one of them why once. The person I asked was an ex-student from the Open University postgraduate systems thinking courses. They said to me: 'Why would I?' Simple as that. They perceived that there was no benefit in showcasing their excellent work to others who generally took no notice of them. They told me that they were too busy getting on with things . When I thought about it, I believe they had a point, although it did stop me in my tracks.

Is it shallow? I do not think so, because systems thinking includes humans and the nature of human behaviour is not shallow. We are the creators and destroyers of ourselves. We create the conditions around us that do not let systems thinking thrive. Why do we prefer competition and winning over sharing and collaborating? Why do we prefer control over freedom? Why do we prefer to only see what we want to see, rather than seeing the bigger picture or a different perspective? These are quite deep questions, and I am sure they are being debated and considered by many across the globe.

In essence, I think the question is the wrong question. Maybe we should be asking, 'If systems thinking is quite obvious, so why is it still largely sitting in the world of the academic without it being practically applied?' It is only with this kind of question, rather than the seemingly everlasting, 'it's great - no it isn't' debate that I think we can move forwards.

The Tinkerbell effect

Despite my inner concerns, I continue to pursue what I believe to be good and right. What I believe is true to human nature and what sets us free from negativity and binding control. It is a tough road to travel, but I have not been put off yet. Sometimes, I wonder if a 'Tinkerbell effect' is at play. You have to see it before you can believe in it.

Chapter 12: My future practice

Out of the wilderness

It is a warm and sleepy Wednesday in August. I am sat at the computer as is usual during the week and yet my world feels different somehow. I felt despondent over the last six months. Lost. Like I no longer belonged to the systems thinking discipline I had dedicated the last sixteen years of my life to. More recently, I had been wandering aimlessly in a wilderness of tiredness and disorientation. It took a new context and a few different pairs of eyes and ears to help me realise that my newfound wilderness was not a wilderness at all but an exciting part of a long overdue pivot into the next place for my systems practice.

More recently, I have met with people who have talked about humility and empathy, consciousness and spirituality and I never thought I would be in deep exploratory conversations about those particular topics. It has been invigorating to be the least experienced in the room. It was as revitalising as standing under a cool waterfall, letting the water cascade over my head, hit my shoulders and run refreshingly down my back. I have gone from feeling exceptionally absent and detached to knowing that I am transitioning. The last systems practice bridge I crossed is behind me and I am staring down the grassy bank towards the next one, feeling the urge to put my foot onto the first unsteady-looking wooden slat. The transition started on my last holiday.

A reset of the mind

It has not been long since I returned from a holiday on the island of Tenerife in the Canaries. I went because I was tired and overwhelmed by what had been happening in the United Kingdom. I personally felt exhausted by our seemingly plummeting humanity, the selfishness, the entitlement and greed, the division that Covid-19, our amoral government and Brexit have brought us. I did not know why at the time because my brain was too tired to process my thoughts, but I had an overwhelming desire to sit at the window seat on the aeroplane. By desire, I mean desperate need. I wanted to look out and see the land, the sea, the sky and the clouds. I wanted to experience our world without the people. I craved this different perspective.

'That's not at all strange,' I hear you say. It was for me, though. I am a bit scared of heights. I tend to get disorientated when looking upwards, so the lack of reference point when looking into the sky can catch me out a bit. For that reason, I do not like it when the plane is climbing and the only direction I can see is up. But this time, I craved to see it with a desperation that came from deep inside. I had to see it, no matter what. I thought about that as I was packing my suitcase more than I thought about the actual holiday itself. It was all-consuming as I prepared to leave the country.

The two years immediately prior to going on holiday were exhausting and turbulent. I worked seven days a week, most weeks and that is not a boast. It was survival. I was incredibly busy working with several clients across different geographical areas, alongside my tutoring and lecturing responsibilities. My holiday was not just a break, it was an essential time of focusing just on myself, to support my wellness. When working with groups of people, sometimes your own welfare can get lost, as the focus is always on the rest of the group. In consultancy that can be amplified as you are not with the same group of people constantly, so lacking mutual two-way support. Add that to the type of emotional load I deal with when working in the arena of systems change, and it is sometimes a heavy weight to bear.

I walked out onto the tarmac at the airport and climbed the metal stairs onto the plane. I could feel the work stress trickling away and I became heavy-eyed and drowsy. I settled into my seat next to the window and made myself comfortable for take-off. As the plane taxiied up to the correct position at the end of the runway, I was calm, my shoulders were slightly slumped and I rested my head on the back of the seat. The feeling was akin to being comfortably settled in my own bed at night. Then, the thrust of the engines kicked in and we were off. I was not brave enough to look out of the window on our ascent, but I did look out for the rest of the journey and had beautiful views of Mount Teide as we approached the volcanic island that would be my home for the next seven days.

The holiday was an absolute joy. Coming home, I got to the airport early, which was normal for me. It is a contingency that reduces the stress of the journey. It was early morning and it was quiet. The taxi driver waved me off with, 'Have a good flight!' and I knew I was going to miss the beautiful volcanic island and its people. I sat for a while in the airport before check-in. I was contemplative, having had some downtime in the sunshine. I got through security like a breeze and went to have a coffee and something to eat. I felt alive inside and yet somewhat subdued. I guess I was just relaxed. I felt confident and had no nervousness about the airport at all. I travel and holiday alone. At first, this used to bring great anxiety but as I formed good habits about contingencies should anything untoward happen, considered and managed my potential risks and learned better ways to manage the transport element I am much more relaxed about it nowadays. In fact, my friends often ask me to holiday with them, but I feel I would be missing the deep contemplative quiet time that I have on my own. I politely refuse and I think they understand. I love being around the pool on my own, listening to music, reading and swimming all day. I like dining alone and savouring my food, focusing on it completely. I especially like the serenity over breakfast as I feast on fresh fruit and hot coffee.

As I stood on the runway waiting to climb the steps onto the plane, I felt a lump in my throat and a tear in my eye. I was not necessarily sad to come home but I was sad because I felt that I needed more quiet contemplative time. I looked around at the airport runway. It was a surrounding that was unfamiliar to me. It was exciting and enticing. The warm air hit my face and my hair blew in the wind. I boarded the plane and was thrilled to find that I was in my window seat with a whole row of seats to myself. The delight! I settled in and looked out of the window again.

I contemplated our plight in the UK, as we prepared for take-off. I spent a few minutes reading and came across some text that made me realise that all we can really do is help those within our reach, no matter how small. If it helps someone, it is useful.

At that moment, I remembered how much wisdom we read and then forget. It helped me regain focus in this overwhelming world. It helped me remember the compassion in the work I do. The conditions I model to support myself and others as we learn and grow.

As we were taking off, I attempted to step into and change my embedded frame of reference about my irrational fear of looking out of the aeroplane window at the world outside. Surprisingly, I managed to re-frame the situation well. I can tell you that the only time I moved my eyes from that window in the whole 4.5 hours of the flight was when I was writing a short story, which popped into my mind and demanded to be written down. My mindset and the contemplative framing had my creative juices flowing and by the time we were halfway home, I had written the full story. I did not even have to think about it. It just poured out of my head, and I thoroughly enjoyed writing it. It was like being inside my very own favourite book. Even then, I wrote a sentence then looked out of the window, and then wrote another. I looked into the sky with no fear at all. I saw the most beautiful planet outside of the window. I felt free and liberated.

I knew I was unbelievably lucky to be experiencing this perspective and I savoured every second. I saw the sea, ships, fields, roads, and trucks. We flew over a wind farm, and I felt excited to see it from above for the very first time. Our world really is an utterly beautiful place. I experienced sadness that sometimes, I can get so wrapped up in my life that I forget to appreciate the world around me. I cannot even express in words how much I appreciated it at that point in time. It brought home to me the importance of different perspectives and framings. Not just perspectives from different people, but different framings that we use ourselves. The lenses we put over our own eyes dictate the way we experience the world. The desperate urge I felt was the urge to change my own embedded framing for something new and fresh.

I believe that reframing is an important skill for practitioners in this complex world. Not just for our work, but for ourselves personally. My mind is now firmly on how I, as a practitioner, can help others to understand the value of this activity and enact it for themselves.

I definitely feel that it is our own self-development where we need to invest the effort moving forward. This goes further than just learning. It is clearly in the self-development camp, and I do not think these two things are quite the same. We can learn things about ourselves but never do anything to change the things we do not like. Developing ourselves and enhancing our own capabilities is a step further. I am already updating my Creating the Conditions for Change materials to reflect self-development, not just learning, but more prominently as a central concept of the approach. It is easy to forget to give our own self-development enough time and effort in this frantic, chaotic world and yet it is vital to enable effective systems practice.

Journeying

The fact that my systems practice journey is taking a new turn has now fully dawned on me. I cannot say I have completely worked out where I am going yet, but I know I am on the next leg of my journey. It is now time for me to put old negative vibes to one side and concentrate on my own exploratory journey again. I collected my luggage and contemplated what was next for me as I drove home. I was acutely aware that I was going to be on a new and probably very different bridge this time around and I was a little unnerved that I had not yet fully sensed which direction it would go in. Sometimes, a practitioner's journey can be like that. We advocate for being comfortable in uncertainty and I now have a very good idea of what that feels like. I need to trust this journey and just let it play out, in the same way I encourage my clients to trust their journeys.

From systems thinking to systems feeling

I feel that I have started to move away from systems thinking to a place of systems feeling and self-development. Am I in a place of systems being? Maybe, but I do not feel I can claim that yet.

Whilst I do not yet know what my future holds, I do know that it is going to be about people, consciousness, the depth of our souls and how we feel and develop ourselves to feel comfortable in this world. This has not been a wholly conscious choice. It has been more like an unconscious guide working from deep inside of me, steering me in this new direction. I have felt it in the very depth of my body for some time and yet I have been unable to articulate it. I did not know what it was. It felt like the snake of love that resided in my stomach a few years ago, except I feel this in every cell of my being. I feel it inside of me and through all of me. It has become me.

My journeys across the bridge to date have felt like a challenging mountain climb. I started out at the bottom of an ominous systems thinking mountain, looking up at the dark rock sides looming over me. I had all the right equipment as I prepared for the climb. After the first leg of my journey, I felt like I was on an exciting expedition that many others had not experienced. I climbed. My arms and legs ached. It was a good ache, though. One that signified growth and strength. I paused when I needed to, took a drink when I needed to and relied on my climbing partners when I needed to. I stopped whenever I could to look around and take in the scenery from my new elevated position. I climbed a bit more. I slipped and fell more than once, scraping my arms and legs and spending days in pain recovering. I carried on. I started to understand how to manoeuvre around the mountain. How to gain traction and where not to put my feet.

It was a unique and challenging journey. Many others had climbed the mountain before me but never had they taken the exact same route I was taking. This was my unique journey. At times it was lonely. At times there were too many people on the mountain at the same time for me to feel comfortable. I clung on, however, and kept going. Then I came to a ledge. It was wide enough for me to sit down and relax, have some food and drink and bask in the sunshine for a while. It was here that I was able to engage in very deep reflections about my work, systems thinking and practice, my life experiences and about the nature of human beings.

I stood up, and, realising I had somehow moved to the edge of the cliff, I felt dazed. My legs wobbled like a newborn deer, staggering around, learning to walk for the first time. I thought I was going to be sick. I grabbed onto the rock face with one hand to steady myself. The world around me was twisting, twirling, whirling. The land and sky blended into one. My eyes became blurred. I tried to turn around to face the mountainside to see if I could focus my gaze and steady myself. The rock face became one giant blur. I turned around and faced the vast landscape ahead of me. The sun was blazing hot, my head was spinning. I tentatively put one foot in front of another. My foot came down on the side of a rock and over I went. I stumbled to my left as I tried to lunge towards my right. My balance failed and I felt myself tipping over the edge. My hands flew above my head, and I fell backwards into the air. I was on my back, falling. It was the free fall of the systems thinking practitioner s journey. It can happen frequently to some of us. I just need to have confidence that, whilst free-falling through the sky, I will somehow have a cushioned landing as I begin the unexpected plunge into something new.

Areas of interest for my future practice

What is this new territory I am exploring? I am up on my feet and wandering around, dazed but excited and energised. I see a pond ahead that I would like to dip my toes into. I have always liked to remain on the edge of my work arenas and dip my toes into several other ponds at the same time. Especially ponds where people think differently from me. I find it intriguing and exciting. I like dipping my toes into a new pond. It tickles my toes and sends a shiver up my spine.

The people I have come across in these new ponds have been deeply inspiring and a catalyst, drawing me into cross-disciplinary work, with a much deeper focus on developing individuals, including myself.

With this in mind, I am contemplating the areas of interest that have brought me joy on the most recent steps of my journey. My tentative steps on a whole new bridge have united me with people and communities who have touched me deep inside, but as yet I have not fully processed why. I am just going along with the flow of this intoxicating journey, trusting where the gently undulating current might take me. I will share with you some of the areas I currently find inspiring. I am already deeply considering and incorporating these into my work, testing out the concepts for myself.

Conscious Leadership

I have recently been delving deeper into conscious leadership. Being self-aware, empathetic and collaborative has always been a feature of my systems practice, so it seems to fit well.

This kind of territory was a gnarly dark forest to me in the past, just as systems change was. The thought of talking about consciousness and being were once concepts that would see me turn away. Over the course of my work and my life, however, they have become more and more prominent in my interests. I suspect the discomfort is that I have a deep interest in them and yet I do not how to process those thoughts in a way that enables me to incorporate them effectively into my working life. I would like to spend my days doing what I love, rather than only dipping into new territories part-time. When I am interested in something, I tend to go all in. I am whole body in, heart and soul. Therefore, it helps if I can make a living along the way, otherwise, I can become discontented with my daily work as my mind is always elsewhere.

My work over the last few years has been very empathy driven. I want to go much further than this. I want to develop it with a foot firmly placed in a new paradigm to see what other insights and revelations it brings. Dare I even say it, I am contemplating what spirituality might mean in all of this if anything. Again, that is not a territory I would have originally gone into, although I understand this is where I now stand.

Wisdom and traditional wisdom

I am only part way down this path and wisdom is something I intend to explore much more fully. I have come across traditional wisdom in my work and I feel there is much, much more that I can learn, and I feel it is right in front of my nose. Wisdom intrigues me. What intrigues me even more, is why we seem to turn away from wisdom and fall into things like capitalism. Indeed, there is an argument about what wisdom truly is and from whose perspective. This is going to be a deep exploration for me. In fact, I think that rabbit hole of communication and information might look like a breeze compared to what this part of my journey could bring up. I shall look forward to scraping my elbows and tripping over my own two feet along the way.

I am particularly interested in the link between wisdom and ethics. How and where are people taught their ethics nowadays as we seem to push wisdom to one side? I am not convinced we get it through the family as much as in the past. I am also not convinced that we get it through religion as much as in the past. These things do exist and influence our ethics of course, although I do think that the influence of deeper wisdom is being lost somewhat. Maybe it is there, but we need to rediscover it by looking in different places. In films, in songs, in stories. Who knows? I am getting my boots on and picking up my torch ready to go down the dark, unfamiliar hole and to see what and who I meet down there.

I know! I know! This is not where I thought I would end up when I started my journey, but here I am. The work of others, and in some respects my own work, is currently turning me upside down and it is disorientating and yet delightful. I am contemplating topics that I would never have contemplated in the past. I am putting out my foot to step onto the next precarious slat of the bridge as I continue on this fresh new adventure.

Onwards

In my work, I have always advocated for strong values and ethics and my intention at this stage of my journey is to be ruthless in my determination for ethics, humility and humanity. The wealth that will be important will not be monetary wealth but experiential wealth. People before money is usually my ethos and I intend to strengthen this further. Taking great care of individuals and focusing on individual development is integral to my Creating the Conditions for Change work and I am building on this by exploring additional topics much more deeply.

Another area that has always been extremely important to me is the idea of gaining excellence in the basics of systems thinking, which I mentioned earlier in this book. Going back to basics and considering how to embody them more deeply, for me, is where the power of anything new lies. It is about embedding the different habits that I have spoken about in previous chapters, and I will be contemplating ways I might support other people and myself to do this even better. I will also be seeking to understand other ways to serve those who I believe could benefit from the value I have to offer. How do I engage with those for whom this work has a deeper meaning and more relevant use? I guess moving forward, my journey will be as much about clearing out as it will be about deeply resetting what I am focusing on. It may even mean a re-set of my own identity to reflect whatever emerges after my next expedition across the bridge and down the rabbit hole.

In short, I appear to be having a reset of my mind as I am moving forward. What I believe I would like to do next is to support myself and others as we develop our deep inner calm and wisdom and connect with our consciousness.

Chapter 13: On never giving up

Despite all of the trips across the bridge, interesting topics, rabbit holes and learning experiences, it can still be really easy to give up, or contemplate giving up, on our systems practice. Sometimes, the challenges seem too big and overwhelming. The lack of support too isolating. The invisibility cloak too smothering and the emotional tidal wave too suffocating. Our habits slip all too easily, back into our old ways and the dance floor can be bitterly competitive. Some people I know, who tried to get to grips with systems practice, gave up in the first few months. They told me that they found it too conceptual, too difficult to get people on board and it can be exhausting to engage with a world that others cannot see or conceptualise.

It can take significant personal investment to keep going on your delicate journey of discovery. It can take an intellectual toll on you, as you push yourself forwards and put yourself into situations that challenge your current mindset. The emotional toll can become too much and drive you to exhaustion. Add to that, the deeply competitive work context, particularly in the UK, and it is sometimes no easy ride. It takes guts and stamina to keep going. I will say it again, it is not for the faint-hearted.

It would have been very easy for me to give up, especially in the last couple of years. I went from believing I was doing the right thing by using the VSM in a rational, empathetic, humble and humanity-driven leadership way, to wanting to walk away from it completely and then back again. I found dealing with the trauma of the Covid-19 pandemic and how that turned our lives upside down extremely challenging. As I mentioned previously, I have also been deeply impacted by our current government and the division driven into our communities. I struggle to watch just how quickly our standard of living has fallen and quite possibly might never be the same again. Not in my lifetime anyway.

I have also contemplated the existential crisis our planet is facing. We have had scorching heat, crazy weather and the decimation of our beautiful natural resources. How could we be so stupid as a species?

In fact, it would have been very easy to give up at several points on my journey. The point where the quicksand around me became all-consuming and I started to sink. The point where I was down so many dark rabbit holes at once that I nearly lost my way. The point when I came across those who were not so ethical, and they cast a dark shadow across my path that I had to navigate. The point where life was so much more attractive outside of the world of systems practice. As a practitioner, our challenges are sometimes plentiful. It is rarely an easy ride and I think it is important to recognise that. Toxic positivity about the discipline helps no one and being realistic and honest about our challenges can help us understand and move past them.

Despite the challenges, I do believe that it is far more beneficial to not give up, even when it feels like you are in an everlasting cage fight, sometimes with yourself. My persistence has seen me venture into places and ideas that I never could have imagined, and I have had an absolute blast in most of them. I have met deeply interesting and inspiring people and developed as a human beyond my wildest expectations. I have come to realise that whilst we are suffering or struggling, in whatever way and for whatever reason, our wisdom is growing. The good more often than not outweighs the bad. One thing that I find particularly special about this field is that it is so broad, that you can take several very interesting turns in your journey and never follow the same path twice. There are also many overlapping ponds where you can live on the edge and dip your toes in without losing a grip on your own discipline. That is one of the reasons I find it so interesting. There is generally always somewhere new to go with it and new experiences to throw yourself into.

My hopes for your journey

I hope that you go well on your journey. On your way, I would urge you to seek out and celebrate enlightened individuals. I have found great strength in listening to and learning from the wisdom of others and I hope you have that experience too. I believe that you do not need shiny toolkits or elaborate approaches that you have no real chance of applying. Share an ethos, not a tool. Look inside yourself for your answers. Trust yourself and your deep instincts. Seek to unlock your inner confidence. Explore what guiding principles work for you and develop strong habits from your own deep insights. Work on them over and over and review and update them along the way. As you venture down the darkened rabbit holes, allow the journey to rekindle your inner wisdom. When you come out of the rabbit hole and find yourself crossing to the other side of the bridge, truly live your narrative. Feel your systems practice as it comes to life deep inside of you. When the wooden slats of the bridge break and the ropes fray, do not lose hope. You will find a way.

I hope for you to explore your inner humility and humanity. I hope you grow and flourish in ways you could never imagine. Your health and wellbeing along the way are your responsibility, do not take them lightly. Be clear about your priorities and I would urge you to consider people first. Do not just talk about your systems practice. Live it. Feel it. Let it represent what you stand for. In my own practice, I have reframed what I do, to focus on personal humility, rationality and ethics. This will not be for everyone. Let your journey guide you wherever you feel you want to go. Who is it you serve? Who is it you would like to serve? What is the purpose of your existence? Most of all, I want to stress that systems thinking and systems practice are for everyone and anyone who is interested. No matter who you are. Whether you work or not. Whether you are rich or poor. Whether you are old or young. It is applicable to everyone equally and everyone's journey is valid and worthy of telling.

Some final words

With that, I want to leave you with some final words. This book was intended as a reflective account of a systems thinking practitioner's learning journey. My journey. As I mentioned in the introduction, I wrote it because I often get asked about the issues and challenges I encounter. I get asked about surviving setbacks and obstacles. I get asked how to keep going in this steeplechase when all we seem to do is get our feet caught on the hurdles and end up face-first in the water. I get asked about the journey more than I get asked about the approaches, models, methods and concepts of systems thinking.

It is my belief that the journey of the practitioner is what makes the discipline so special. It is the story less told and yet I believe it is the most powerful story. It is the story of how and why we form our habits. What resonated for us along the way and what did not. What helped us to change, what did not. It is a journey like no other and each person's journey is unique. Mine has been a journey of revelation and on more than one occasion it has been a journey of deep inner reflection and personal transformation. It has enabled me to learn more about life than anything else I have encountered. For that reason, it has been, and continues to be, a journey of continual healing from the hurt in our world and a journey of hope.

Out of trauma, comes wisdom.

Out of fear, comes hope.

Out of distress, comes calm.

Out of battle, comes peace.

Out of death, comes life.

Out of disorientation, comes transformation.

Crossing the Bridge

Out of darkness, comes enlightenment.

Our explorations can bring us hope.

As a human, I have learnt how to relax and flow along in the peace of the undulating river of my systems practice, and I hope it is the same for you. Let it take you to where you need to be, even if you do not know where that is. Trust life. Your journey might be turbulent. It might be sad. It might be difficult. It might also be lively and happy and warm. It might be inspiring and enlightening. It might be joyful. It is very likely to be all of these, wrapped up in a repeating cycle. How you use the opportunities that each cycle brings, is entirely up to you. I believe each cycle is a massive opportunity for personal development and growth. Importantly, it is YOUR story to write. Not someone else's. If you do not like the journey at one point in time, go in a different direction. There are always opportunities for something different if need be. Most importantly, and I urge you most sincerely, to never give up.

Glossary

Ashby's law of requisite variety – Only variety can destroy variety. This means that a variety in the regulator of a system must be as great as the variety in the system.

Boundary judgements – Judgements that are explicitly or implicitly made about understanding situations and guiding actions in situations.

Causal loop diagram – diagrams that show circular causes and effects in situations.

Critical Systems Heuristics – a systems thinking approach developed by Werner Ulrich. It renders messy situations as a reference system, exploring four sources of influence – motivation, control, knowledge and legitimacy.

Double loop learning – when our learning involves questioning the purposes of our actions.

Feedback – circular interconnectivity that is present in situations.

Feedback loop – a way of representing the circular interconnectivity in situations.

Management cybernetics – defined by Stafford Beer as the science of effective organisation.

Pharmaceutical specials – bespoke pharmaceutical medicinal products, made by hand.

Prototyping – an early sample of something used to test out a concept or a process.

Reframing – an act of adjusting your mindset.

Rich picture – a diagram that represents a complex situation in pictures.

Soft systems methodology – a systems thinking approach developed by Peter Checkland. It is centred on developing purposeful activity models.

Structural coupling – the way a complex system adjusts its structure to the environment. It involves the constant interaction between the system and its environment.

System blindness – blind spots we have when observing situations.

System Dynamics – a modelling based approach to understand the behaviour of complex systems.

Systemic inquiry – an inquiry using systems concepts and ideas.

System pathology – a pattern of behaviour that is common in systems.

Systems change – a largely contested term. Generally concerned with system level interventions to make change.

Systems thinking practitioner – someone who puts the craft and skills of systems thinking into practice.

Triple loop learning – this is where our learning supports us to question our own decisions that frame our actions.

Viable System Model – a model designed by Stafford Beer outlining sufficient and necessary characteristics required for viability.

Vicious cycle – reinforcing feedback loops that create an unwelcome change.

Virtuous cycle – reinforcing feedback loops that create a welcome change.

References

Beer S. (1981) *Brain of the Firm. Second Edition.* Chichester. John Wiley & Sons Inc.

Beer S. (1985) *Diagnosing the System for Organisations.* Chichester. John Wiley & Sons Inc.

Frederickson, Barbara L. (2013) *Love 2.0. How our supreme emotion affects everything we feel, think, do and become.* New York. Hudson Street Press.

Lieberman, Matthew D. (2013) *Social, why our brains are wired to connect.* Oxford. Oxford University Press.

(2019) Manhunt, Series 1, episodes 1-3 & Series 2, episodes 1-4 ITV. Available at ITVX https://www.itv.com/watch/manhunt/2a5386/2a5386a0001

Maturana, H, Verden-Zoller, R, Verden-Zoller, G. (2008) *The Origin of Humanness in the Biology of Love.* Imprint academic.

McChrystal, S. (2015) *Team of Teams. New rules of engagement for a complex world.* UK and USA, Penguin Random House.

Morgan, G. (1998) *Riding the Waves of Change. Developing Managerial Competencies for a Turbulent World.* London. Jossey-Bass Publishers.

Navaro, J. (2021) *Be Exceptional: Master the Five Traits that Set Extraordinary People Apart* New York. Harper Collins.

Wheatley, Margaret J and Kellner-Rogers, Myron (1996) *A Simpler Way*, San Francisco Barrett-Koehler Publishers.

Printed in Great Britain
by Amazon

50431617R00119